# WORKING PAPERS

*to accompany*

# ACCOUNTING PRINCIPLES

***5th Edition***

## VOLUME 1 / CHAPTERS 1-13

**JERRY J. WEYGANDT** Ph.D., C.P.A.
Arthur Andersen Alumni Professor of Accounting
University of Wisconsin - Madison
Madison, Wisconsin

**DONALD E. KIESO** Ph.D., C.P.A.
KPMG Peat Marwick Emeritus Professor of Accounting
Northern Illinois University
DeKalb, Illinois

**PAUL D. KIMMEL** Ph.D., C.P.A.
Associate Professor of Accounting
University of Wisconsin - Milwaukee
Milwaukee, Wisconsin

**Prepared By**
**ANNE LEE BAIN** M.A., C.P.A.
Assistant Professor of Accounting
St. Cloud State University
St. Cloud, Minnesota

**JOHN WILEY & SONS, INC.**
New York • Chichester • Weinheim • Brisbane • Singapore • Toronto

COVER PHOTO © Paul Souders/Tony Stone Images, New York



ISBN 0-471-19443-3

Printed in the United States of America

10 9 8 7 6 5 4 3 2 1

Printed and bound by Courier Stoughton, Inc.

# NOTE TO THE STUDENT

These working papers contain solution forms for all Brief Exercises, Exercises, and Problems in Weygandt et al., *Accounting Principles*, 5th edn., chapters 1–13 and Appendix D. From the "Broadening Your Perspective" section at the end of each chapter, the working papers also contain solution forms for each Financial Reporting Problem, Comparative Analysis Problem, Financial Statement Interpretation, Real-World Focus, Group Decision Case, and Ethics Case. Because the solutions to the remaining "Broadening Your Perspective" problems tend to be free-form, there are no working papers for any of the problems entitled "Research Assignment," "Communication Activity," or "Surfing the Net." There are, likewise, no working paper solution forms for any of the Self-Study Questions or chapter Questions at the end of each chapter.

In general, the working papers follow the organization of the textbook. To maximize the use of space, however, forms for the Exercises occasionally appear out of order and the Real-World Focus and Ethics Case solution forms frequently appear on the same page at the end of each chapter's working papers. And several problems for Chapter 4 (P4- 1A, P4-4A, P4-5A, P4-6A, P4-1B, P4-4B, and P4-5B), Chapter 5 (P5-3A and P5-3B), and the Chapter 6 Financial Reporting Problem (Mini-Practice Set), and Appendix D (P D-1, P D-2, and P D-3) require 11" x 17" sheets, which are separately bound in the back of this volume.

Name

Section

Date

Name
Section
Date

Name **Exercises 1-1 to 1-3**

Section

Date

**#1**

**#2**

**#3**

 

Name

Section

Date

**Exercise 1-4**

**Maria Mendoza & Co.**

(a)

(b)

(c)

Name

Section

Date

**Exercise 1-5**

**Maria Mendoza & Co.**

Name

Section

Date

**Exercise 1-6**

**Dylan Company**

(a)

(b)

(c)

Name

Section

Date

**Exercise 1-7**

**Anne Wyatt, D.D.S., & Rambo Enterprises**

(a)

(b)

(c)

(d)

Name

Section

Date

**Exercise 1-8**

**Dyna Jeng Co.**

Name

Section

Date

#9

#10

Name

Section

Date

**Exercises 1-11 to 1-12**

**#11**

**#12**

Name
Section
Date

**Problem 1-1A**

**Wayne State Travel Agency**

(a)

WAYNE STATE TRAVEL AGENCY

| | Assets | | | | = | Liabilities | + | Owner's Equity |
|---|---|---|---|---|---|---|---|---|
| Transactions | Cash | + Accounts Receivable | + Supplies | + Office Equipment | = | Accounts Payable | + | Merle Peper Capital |
| 1. | | | | | | | | |
| 2. | | | | | | | | |
| 3. | | | | | | | | |
| 4. | | | | | | | | |
| 5. | | | | | | | | |
| 6. | | | | | | | | |
| 7. | | | | | | | | |
| 8. | | | | | | | | |
| 9. | | | | | | | | |
| 10. | | | | | | | | |

Name

Section

Date

**Problem 1-1A Concluded**

**Wayne State Travel Agency**

(b)

Name

Section

Date





(a)

## GEORGE KANAAN, ATTORNEY AT LAW

| | Assets | | | | | | | = | Liabilities | | | + | Owner's Equity |
|---|---|---|---|---|---|---|---|---|---|---|---|---|---|
| Trans-action | Cash | + | Accounts Receivable | + | Supplies | + | Office Equipment | = | Notes Payable | + | Accounts Payable | + | George Kanaan, Capital |
| Bal. | $4,000 | + | $1,500 | + | $500 | + | $5,000 | = | | + | $4,200 | + | $6,800 |
| 1. | | | | | | | | | | | | | |
| 2. | | | | | | | | | | | | | |
| 3. | | | | | | | | | | | | | |
| 4. | | | | | | | | | | | | | |
| 5. | | | | | | | | | | | | | |
| 6. | | | | | | | | | | | | | |
| 7. | | | | | | | | | | | | | |
| 8. | | | | | | | | | | | | | |

(b)

GEORGE KANAAN, ATTORNEY AT LAW
Income Statement
For the Month Ended August 31, 1999

Revenues

Expenses

Net Income (loss)

GEORGE KANAAN, ATTORNEY AT LAW
Owner's Equity Statement
For the Month Ended August 31, 1999

Name
Section
Date



(b) (Continued)

GEORGE KANAAN, ATTORNEY AT LAW
Balance Sheet
August 31, 1999

| | |
|---|---|
| Assets | |
| | |
| | |
| | |
| | |
| | |
| | |
| | |
| | |
| | |
| Liabilities and Owner's Equity | |

Name

Section

Date

**Problem 1-3A**

**Secret Cosmetics Co.**

(a)

SECRET COSMETICS CO.
Income Statement
For the Month Ended June 30, 1999

Revenues

Expenses

Net Income (loss)

SECRET COSMETICS CO.
Owner's Equity Statement
For the Month Ended June 30, 1999

Name

Section

Date

**Problem 1-3A Continued**

**Secret Cosmetics Co.**

(a) (Continued)

SECRET COSMETICS CO.
Balance Sheet
June 30, 1999

| | |
|---|---|
| Assets | |
| Liabilities and Owner's Equity | |

(b)

SECRET COSMETICS CO.
Income Statement
For the Month Ended June 30, 1999

| | |
|---|---|
| Revenues | |
| Expenses | |
| Net Income (loss) | |

(b) (Continued)

SECRET COSMETICS CO.
Owner's Equity Statement
For the Month Ended June 30, 1999

Name

Section

Date

**Problem 1-4A**

**Bell Consulting**

(a)

| Date | Assets | | | | = | Liabilities | | + | Owner' Equity | |
|---|---|---|---|---|---|---|---|---|---|---|
| | Cash | + Accounts Receivable | + Supplies | + Office Equipment | = | Notes Payable | + Accounts Payable | + | J. Bell, Capital | Explanation |
| May 1 | | | | | | | | | | |
| 2 | | | | | | | | | | |
| 3 | | | | | | | | | | |
| 5 | | | | | | | | | | |
| 9 | | | | | | | | | | |
| 12 | | | | | | | | | | |
| 15 | | | | | | | | | | |
| 17 | | | | | | | | | | |
| 20 | | | | | | | | | | |
| 23 | | | | | | | | | | |
| 26 | | | | | | | | | | |
| 29 | | | | | | | | | | |
| 30 | | | | | | | | | | |
| | | | | | | | | | | |

(b)

BELL CONSULTING
Income Statement
For the Month Ended May 31, 1999

| | | |
|---|---|---|
| Revenues | | |
| | | |
| | | |
| Expenses | | |
| | | |
| | | |
| | | |
| | | |
| | | |
| | | |
| | | |
| Net income | | |
| | | |
| | | |

(c)

BELL CONSULTING
Balance Statement
May 31, 1999

| | | |
|---|---|---|
| Assets | | |
| | | |
| | | |
| | | |
| | | |
| | | |
| Liabilities and Owner's Equity | | |
| | | |
| | | |
| | | |
| | | |
| | | |
| | | |
| | | |

Name

Section

Date

**Problem 1-5A**

**Montreal Company and Others**

(a)

| | Montreal Company | Calgary Company | Edmonton Company | Vancouver Company |
|---|---|---|---|---|

(b) and (c)

(b)

MONTREAL COMPANY

Owner's Equity Statement

For the Year Ended December 31, 1999

(c)

Name

Section

Date

**Problem 1-1B**

**Kumar's Repair Shop**

(a)

KUMAR'S REPAIR SHOP

| Transactions | Assets: Cash | + | Accounts Receivable | + | Supplies | + | Equipment | = | Liabilities: Accounts Payable | + | Owner's Equity: U. Kumar, Capital |
|---|---|---|---|---|---|---|---|---|---|---|---|
| 1. | | | | | | | | | | | |
| 2. | | | | | | | | | | | |
| 3. | | | | | | | | | | | |
| 4. | | | | | | | | | | | |
| 5. | | | | | | | | | | | |
| 6. | | | | | | | | | | | |
| 7. | | | | | | | | | | | |
| 8. | | | | | | | | | | | |
| 9. | | | | | | | | | | | |
| 10. | | | | | | | | | | | |
| 11. | | | | | | | | | | | |

Name

Section

Date

**Problem 1-1B Concluded**

**Kumar's Repair Shop**

(b)

Name

Section

Date

**Problem 1-2B**

**Bruce Smith, Veterinarian**

(a)

BRUCE SMITH, VETERINARIAN

| | Assets | | | | | | | = | Liabilities | | | + | Owner's Equity |
|---|---|---|---|---|---|---|---|---|---|---|---|---|---|
| Trans-actions | Cash | + | Accounts Receivable | + | Supplies | + | Office Equipment | = | Notes Payable | + | Accounts Payable | + | Bruce Smith, Capital |
| Bal. | $9,000 | + | $1,700 | + | $600 | + | $6,000 | = | | + | $3,600 | + | $13,700 |
| 1. | | | | | | | | | | | | | |
| | | | | | | | | | | | | | |
| 2. | | | | | | | | | | | | | |
| | | | | | | | | | | | | | |
| 3. | | | | | | | | | | | | | |
| | | | | | | | | | | | | | |
| 4. | | | | | | | | | | | | | |
| | | | | | | | | | | | | | |
| 5. | | | | | | | | | | | | | |
| | | | | | | | | | | | | | |
| 6. | | | | | | | | | | | | | |
| | | | | | | | | | | | | | |
| 7. | | | | | | | | | | | | | |
| | | | | | | | | | | | | | |
| 8. | | | | | | | | | | | | | |
| | | | | | | | | | | | | | |

(b)

BRUCE SMITH, VETERINARIAN

Income Statement

For the Month Ended September 30, 1999

Revenues

Expenses

Net Income (loss)

BRUCE SMITH, VETERINARIAN

Owner's Equity Statement

For the Month Ended September 30, 1999

(b) (Continued)

BRUCE SMITH, VETERINARIAN
Balance Sheet
September 30, 1999

Assets

Liabilities and Owner's Equity

 

Name

Section

Date

**Problem 1-3B**

**Ruston Flying School**

(a)

RUSTON FLYING SCHOOL
Income Statement
For the Month Ended May 31, 1999

| | |
|---|---|
| Revenues | |
| | |
| | |
| | |
| Expenses | |
| | |
| | |
| | |
| | |
| | |
| | |
| | |
| | |
| Net Income (loss) | |
| | |
| | |
| | |
| | |
| | |
| | |

RUSTON FLYING SCHOOL
Owner's Equity Statement
For the Month Ended May 31, 1999

| | |
|---|---|
| | |
| | |
| | |
| | |
| | |
| | |
| | |
| | |
| | |
| | |
| | |
| | |
| | |
| | |
| | |

Name

Section

Date

**Problem 1-3B Continued**

**Ruston Flying School**

(a) (Continued)

RUSTON FLYING SCHOOL

Balance Sheet

May 31, 1999

| | |
|---|---|
| Assets | |
| | |
| | |
| | |
| | |
| | |
| | |
| | |
| | |
| Liabilities and Owner's Equity | |
| | |
| | |
| | |
| | |
| | |
| | |
| | |
| | |
| | |
| | |

(b)

RUSTON FLYING SCHOOL

Income Statement

For the Month Ended May 31, 1999

| | |
|---|---|
| Revenues | |
| | |
| | |
| Expenses | |
| | |
| | |
| | |
| | |
| | |
| | |
| | |
| Net Income (loss) | |
| | |
| | |
| | |

(b) (Continued)

RUSTON FLYING SCHOOL
Owner's Equity Statement
For the Month Ended May 31, 1999

Name

Section

Date

**Problem 1-4B**

**Alex Deliveries**

(a)

| Date | Assets | | | | = | Liabilities | | + | Owner' Equity | |
|---|---|---|---|---|---|---|---|---|---|---|
| | Cash + | Accounts Receivable + | Supplies + | Delivery Van | = | Notes Payable + | Accounts Payable | + | P. Alex, Capital | Explanation |
| May 1 | | | | | | | | | | |
| 2 | | | | | | | | | | |
| 3 | | | | | | | | | | |
| 5 | | | | | | | | | | |
| 9 | | | | | | | | | | |
| 12 | | | | | | | | | | |
| 15 | | | | | | | | | | |
| 17 | | | | | | | | | | |
| 20 | | | | | | | | | | |
| 23 | | | | | | | | | | |
| 26 | | | | | | | | | | |
| 29 | | | | | | | | | | |
| 30 | | | | | | | | | | |

(b)

ALEX DELIVERIES

Income Statement

For the Month Ended June 30, 1999

| | |
|---|---|
| Revenues | |
| | |
| | |
| Expenses | |
| Net income | |

(c)

ALEX DELIVERIES

Balance Statement

June 30, 1999

| | |
|---|---|
| Assets | |
| | |
| Liabilities and Owner's Equity | |
| | |

Name **Problem 1-5B**

Section

Date **Marshall Company and Others**

(a)

| | Loyola Company | Marshall Company | UNLV Company | UNC Company |
|---|---|---|---|---|

(b) and (c)

(b)

MARSHALL COMPANY

Owner's Equity Statement

For the Year Ended December 31, 1999

(c)

Name

Section

Date

**Chapter 1 Financial Reporting Problem**

**Kellogg Company**

(a)

(b)

(c)

(d) Net sales—1995 (in thousands)

1996 (in thousands)

1997 (in thousands)

(e)

| (a) (In millions) | General Mills | Kellogg |
|---|---|---|
| 1. Total assets | | |
| 2. Accounts receivable | | |
| 3. Net sales | | |
| 4. Net income | | |

(b)

 

Name

Section

Date

**Lincoln Village Properties**

Assets

Cash

Accounts receivable

Machinery and Equipment, net

Other noncurrent assets

Total assets

Calculations

(a) Cash

(b) Accounts receivable

(c) Machinery and Equipment, net

(d) Other noncurrent assets

Name **Chapter 1 Group Decision Case**

Section

Date **Long-Shot Driving Range**

(a)

(b)

LONG-SHOT DRIVING RANGE

Balance Sheet

March 31,1999

Assets

Liabilities and Owner's Equity

Name

Section

Date



(c) and (d)

(c)

(d)

Name

Section

Date



**REAL-WORLD FOCUS** Air Transportation Holding Company

(a)

(b)

(c)

**ETHICS CASE** Steve Pelli, Job Interviewee

(a)

(b)

(c)

Name



Section

Date

Name

Section

Date

Name ____________________

Section ____________________

Date ____________________

General Journal

| Date | Account Titles and Explanation | Ref. | Debit | Credit |
|---|---|---|---|---|

| Date | Explanation | Ref. | Debit | Credit | Balance |
|---|---|---|---|---|---|

| Date | Explanation | Ref. | Debit | Credit | Balance |
|---|---|---|---|---|---|

| Date | Explanation | Ref. | Debit | Credit | Balance |
|---|---|---|---|---|---|

Name



Section

Date

Name Exercise 2-1

Section

Date L. Visser, Interior Decorator

| Transaction Date | Account Debited (a) Basic Type | Account Debited (b) Specific Account | Account Debited (c) Effect | Account Debited (d) Normal Balance | Account Credited (a) Basic Type | Account Credited (b) Specific Account | Account Credited (c) Effect | Account Credited (d) Normal Balance |
|---|---|---|---|---|---|---|---|---|
| Jan. | | | | | | | | |
| 2 | Asset | Cash | Increase | Debit | Owner's | L. Visser, | Increase | Credit |
| | | | | | Equity | Capital | | |
| 3 | | | | | | | | |
| 9 | | | | | | | | |
| 11 | | | | | | | | |
| 16 | | | | | | | | |
| 20 | | | | | | | | |
| 23 | | | | | | | | |
| 28 | | | | | | | | |

Name **Exercise 2-2**

Section

Date **L. Visser, Interior Decorator**

General Journal

| | Date | Account Titles and Explanation | Ref. | Debit | Credit | |
|---|---|---|---|---|---|---|
| 1 | | | | | | 1 |
| 2 | | | | | | 2 |
| 3 | | | | | | 3 |
| 4 | | | | | | 4 |
| 5 | | | | | | 5 |
| 6 | | | | | | 6 |
| 7 | | | | | | 7 |
| 8 | | | | | | 8 |
| 9 | | | | | | 9 |
| 10 | | | | | | 10 |
| 11 | | | | | | 11 |
| 12 | | | | | | 12 |
| 13 | | | | | | 13 |
| 14 | | | | | | 14 |
| 15 | | | | | | 15 |
| 16 | | | | | | 16 |
| 17 | | | | | | 17 |
| 18 | | | | | | 18 |
| 19 | | | | | | 19 |
| 20 | | | | | | 20 |
| 21 | | | | | | 21 |
| 22 | | | | | | 22 |
| 23 | | | | | | 23 |
| 24 | | | | | | 24 |
| 25 | | | | | | 25 |
| 26 | | | | | | 26 |
| 27 | | | | | | 27 |
| 28 | | | | | | 28 |
| 29 | | | | | | 29 |
| 30 | | | | | | 30 |
| 31 | | | | | | 31 |
| 32 | | | | | | 32 |
| 33 | | | | | | 33 |
| 34 | | | | | | 34 |
| 35 | | | | | | 35 |
| 36 | | | | | | 36 |
| 37 | | | | | | 37 |
| 38 | | | | | | 38 |
| 39 | | | | | | 39 |
| 40 | | | | | | 40 |

Name

Section

Date

**Exercises 2-3 to 2-4**

**Stine Real Estate Agency**

**#3**

**#4**

| Date | Account Titles and Explanation | Ref. | Debit | Credit |
|---|---|---|---|---|

Name | **Exercise 2-5**
Section
Date | **J. L. Meche, Investment Broker**

(a)

| CASH | | NOTES PAYABLE | |
|---|---|---|---|
| | | | |

| ACCOUNTS RECEIVABLE | | J. L. MECHE, CAPITAL | |
|---|---|---|---|
| | | | |

| OFFICE EQUIPMENT | | SERVICE REVENUE | |
|---|---|---|---|
| | | | |

(b)

J. L. MECHE, INVESTMENT BROKER
Trial Balance
August 31, 1999

| | Debit | Credit |
|---|---|---|
| | | |
| | | |
| | | |
| | | |
| | | |
| | | |
| | | |
| | | |
| | | |
| | | |

Name

Section

Date

**Exercise 2-6**

**Doty Landscaping Company**

(a)

General Journal

| Date | Account Titles and Explanation | Ref. | Debit | Credit |
|---|---|---|---|---|

(b)

DOTY LANDSCAPING COMPANY
Trial Balance
April 30, 1999

| | Debit | Credit |
|---|---|---|

Name

Section

Date

**Exercise 2-7**

**McBride Co.**

(a)

General Journal

| | Date | Account Titles and Explanation | Ref. | Debit | Credit | |
|---|---|---|---|---|---|---|
| 1 | | | | | | 1 |
| 2 | | | | | | 2 |
| 3 | | | | | | 3 |
| 4 | | | | | | 4 |
| 5 | | | | | | 5 |
| 6 | | | | | | 6 |
| 7 | | | | | | 7 |
| 8 | | | | | | 8 |
| 9 | | | | | | 9 |
| 10 | | | | | | 10 |
| 11 | | | | | | 11 |
| 12 | | | | | | 12 |
| 13 | | | | | | 13 |
| 14 | | | | | | 14 |
| 15 | | | | | | 15 |
| 16 | | | | | | 16 |
| 17 | | | | | | 17 |
| 18 | | | | | | 18 |
| 19 | | | | | | 19 |
| 20 | | | | | | 20 |
| 21 | | | | | | 21 |
| 22 | | | | | | 22 |

(b)

McBRIDE CO.
Trial Balance
October 31, 1999

| | | Debit | Credit | |
|---|---|---|---|---|
| 1 | | | | 1 |
| 2 | | | | 2 |
| 3 | | | | 3 |
| 4 | | | | 4 |
| 5 | | | | 5 |
| 6 | | | | 6 |
| 7 | | | | 7 |
| 8 | | | | 8 |
| 9 | | | | 9 |
| 10 | | | | 10 |
| 11 | | | | 11 |
| 12 | | | | 12 |
| 13 | | | | 13 |

Name

Section

Date

**Exercise 2-8**

**Tracy Lawrence Company**

(a)

General Journal J1

| | Date | Account Titles and Explanation | Ref. | Debit | Credit | |
|---|---|---|---|---|---|---|
| 1 | | | | | | 1 |
| 2 | | | | | | 2 |
| 3 | | | | | | 3 |
| 4 | | | | | | 4 |
| 5 | | | | | | 5 |
| 6 | | | | | | 6 |
| 7 | | | | | | 7 |
| 8 | | | | | | 8 |
| 9 | | | | | | 9 |
| 10 | | | | | | 10 |
| 11 | | | | | | 11 |
| 12 | | | | | | 12 |

(b)

Cash No. 101

| Date | Explanation | Ref. | Debit | Credit | Balance |
|---|---|---|---|---|---|
| | | | | | |
| | | | | | |
| | | | | | |
| | | | | | |

Equipment No. 157

| Date | Explanation | Ref. | Debit | Credit | Balance |
|---|---|---|---|---|---|
| | | | | | |
| | | | | | |

Accounts Payable No. 201

| Date | Explanation | Ref. | Debit | Credit | Balance |
|---|---|---|---|---|---|
| | | | | | |
| | | | | | |
| | | | | | |

Tracy Lawrence, Capital No. 301

| Date | Explanation | Ref. | Debit | Credit | Balance |
|---|---|---|---|---|---|
| | | | | | |
| | | | | | |

Tracy Lawrence, Drawing No. 306

| Date | Explanation | Ref. | Debit | Credit | Balance |
|---|---|---|---|---|---|
| | | | | | |
| | | | | | |

Name

Section

Date



**#9**

| Error | (a) In Balance? | (b) Difference | (c) Larger Column |
|---|---|---|---|
| 1. Credit posting of $400 to Accounts Receivable was omitted | No | $400 | Debit |
| 2. | | | |
| 3. | | | |
| 4. | | | |
| 5. | | | |
| 6. | | | |

**#10**

ALWAYS LATE DELIVERY SERVICE
Trial Balance
July 31, 1999

| | Debit | Credit |
|---|---|---|

Name

Section

Date

**Problem 2-1A**

**Four Oaks Miniature Golf and Driving Range**

General Journal

J1

| Date | Account Titles and Explanation | Ref. | Debit | Credit |
|---|---|---|---|---|

Name

Section

Date

**Problem 2-1A Concluded**

**Four Oaks Miniature Golf and Driving Range**

General Journal J2

| Date | Account Titles and Explanation | Ref. | Debit | Credit |
|---|---|---|---|---|

Name

Section

Date

**Problem 2-2A**

**Maria Rojas, Architect**

(a) General Journal J1

| Date | Account Titles and Explanation | Ref. | Debit | Credit |
|---|---|---|---|---|
| | | | | |

Name

Section

Date

**Problem 2-2A Continued**

**Maria Rojas, Architect**

(b)

Cash — No. 101

| Date | Explanation | Ref. | Debit | Credit | Balance |
|---|---|---|---|---|---|
| | | | | | |
| | | | | | |
| | | | | | |
| | | | | | |
| | | | | | |
| | | | | | |
| | | | | | |

Accounts Receivable — No. 112

| Date | Explanation | Ref. | Debit | Credit | Balance |
|---|---|---|---|---|---|
| | | | | | |
| | | | | | |
| | | | | | |

Supplies — No. 126

| Date | Explanation | Ref. | Debit | Credit | Balance |
|---|---|---|---|---|---|
| | | | | | |
| | | | | | |
| | | | | | |

Accounts Payable — No. 201

| Date | Explanation | Ref. | Debit | Credit | Balance |
|---|---|---|---|---|---|
| | | | | | |
| | | | | | |
| | | | | | |
| | | | | | |

Revenue — No. 205

| Date | Explanation | Ref. | Debit | Credit | Balance |
|---|---|---|---|---|---|
| | | | | | |
| | | | | | |
| | | | | | |

Maria Rojas, Capital — No. 301

| Date | Explanation | Ref. | Debit | Credit | Balance |
|---|---|---|---|---|---|
| | | | | | |
| | | | | | |
| | | | | | |

Name | **Problem 2-2A Concluded**

Section

Date | **Maria Rojas, Architect**

(b) (Continued)

Service Revenue — No. 400

| Date | Explanation | Ref. | Debit | Credit | Balance |
|---|---|---|---|---|---|
| | | | | | |
| | | | | | |
| | | | | | |

Salaries Expense — No. 726

| Date | Explanation | Ref. | Debit | Credit | Balance |
|---|---|---|---|---|---|
| | | | | | |
| | | | | | |
| | | | | | |

Rent Expense — No. 729

| Date | Explanation | Ref. | Debit | Credit | Balance |
|---|---|---|---|---|---|
| | | | | | |
| | | | | | |
| | | | | | |

(c)

MARIA ROJAS, ARCHITECT
Trial Balance
April 30, 1999

| | | Debit | Credit | |
|---|---|---|---|---|
| 1 | Cash | | | 1 |
| 2 | Accounts Receivable | | | 2 |
| 3 | Supplies | | | 3 |
| 4 | Accounts Payable | | | 4 |
| 5 | Unearned Revenue | | | 5 |
| 6 | Maria Rojas, Capital | | | 6 |
| 7 | Service Revenue | | | 7 |
| 8 | Salaries Expense | | | 8 |
| 9 | Rent Expense | | | 9 |
| 10 | | | | 10 |
| 11 | | | | 11 |

Name

Section

Date

**Problem 2-3A**

**Judy's Laundry**

(a) and (c)

Cash — No. 101

| Date | Explanation | Ref. | Debit | Credit | Balance |
|---|---|---|---|---|---|
| Oct 1 | Balance | 101 | | | 8500 |
| 5 | | J1 | 800 | | 9300 |
| 15 | | J1 | | 1200 | 8100 |
| 20 | | J1 | | 1600 | 6500 |
| 29 | | J1 | | 500 | 6000 |
| 31 | | J1 | | 500 | 5500 |
| | | | | | |

Accounts Receivable — No. 112

| Date | Explanation | Ref. | Debit | Credit | Balance |
|---|---|---|---|---|---|
| 10/1 | Balance | 112 | | | 2200 |
| 10/5 | | J1 | | 800 | 1400 |
| 10/10 | | J1 | 5500 | | 6900 |
| | | | | | |

Supplies — No. 126

| Date | Explanation | Ref. | Debit | Credit | Balance |
|---|---|---|---|---|---|
| 10/1 | Balance | 126 | | | 1700 |
| | | | | | |

Equipment — No. 157

| Date | Explanation | Ref. | Debit | Credit | Balance |
|---|---|---|---|---|---|
| 10/1 | Balance | 157 | | | 8000 |
| | | | | | |

Accounts Payable — No. 201

| Date | Explanation | Ref. | Debit | Credit | Balance |
|---|---|---|---|---|---|
| 10/1 | Balance | 201 | | | 5000 |
| 10/20 | | | 1600 | | 3400 |
| | | | | | |

Unearned Revenue — No. 206

| Date | Explanation | Ref. | Debit | Credit | Balance |
|---|---|---|---|---|---|
| 10/1 | Balance | 206 | | | 700 |
| | | | | | |
| | | | | | |

Name | **Problem 2-3A Continued**
Section
Date | **Judy's Laundry**

(a) and (c) (Continued)

Judy Kylie, Capital — No. 301

| Date | Explanation | Ref. | Debit | Credit | Balance |
|---|---|---|---|---|---|
| 10/1 | Balance | 301 | | | 14700 |
| | | | | | |

Judy Kylie, Drawing — No. 306

| Date | Explanation | Ref. | Debit | Credit | Balance |
|---|---|---|---|---|---|
| 29 | | J1 | 500 | | 500 |
| | | | | | |

Laundry Revenue — No. 426

| Date | Explanation | Ref. | Debit | Credit | Balance |
|---|---|---|---|---|---|
| 10/10 | | J1 | | 5500 | 5500 |
| | | | | | |
| | | | | | |

Salaries Expense — No. 726

| Date | Explanation | Ref. | Debit | Credit | Balance |
|---|---|---|---|---|---|
| 10/15 | | J1 | 1200 | | 1200 |
| | | | | | |

Utilities Expense — No. 732

| Date | Explanation | Ref. | Debit | Credit | Balance |
|---|---|---|---|---|---|
| | | 732 | | | |
| 31 | | J1 | 500 | | 500 |

(d)

JUDY'S LAUNDRY
Trial Balance
October 31, 1999

| | | Debit | Credit | |
|---|---|---|---|---|
| 1 | Cash | 5500 | | 1 |
| 2 | Accounts Receivable | 6900 | | 2 |
| 3 | Supplies | 1700 | | 3 |
| 4 | Equipment | 8000 | | 4 |
| 5 | Accounts Payable | | 3400 | 5 |
| 6 | Unearned Revenue | | 700 | 6 |
| 7 | Judy Kylie, Capital | | 14700 | 7 |
| 8 | Judy Kylie, Drawing | 500 | | 8 |
| 9 | Laundry Revenue | | 5500 | 9 |
| 10 | Salaries Expense | 1200 | | 10 |
| 11 | Utilities Expense | 500 | | 11 |
| 12 | | | | 12 |
| 13 | | | | 13 |
| | | 24300 | 24300 | |

Name

Section

Date

**Problem 2-3A Concluded**

**Judy's Laundry**

(b)

General Journal

J1

| Date | Account Titles and Explanation | Ref. | Debit | Credit |
|---|---|---|---|---|
| 10/5 | Cash | 101 | 800 | |
| | A/R | 112 | | 800 |
| 10/10 | A/R | 112 | 5500 | |
| | Laundry Rev | 426 | | 5500 |
| 15 | Salary Exp | | 1200 | |
| | Cash | | | 1200 |
| 20 | A/P | | 1600 | |
| | Cash | | | 1600 |
| 29 | Drawing | | 500 | |
| | Cash | | | 500 |
| 31 | Utilities expense | | 500 | |
| | Cash | | | 500 |

Name

Section

Date

**Problem 2-4A**

**Tim Winan Co.**

TIM WINAN CO.
Trial Balance
June 30, 1999

| | Debit | Credit |
|---|---|---|
| | | |
| Journal Entry Aids: | | |
| | | |

Name

Section

Date

**Problem 2-5A**

**Starlite Theater**

(a) and (c)

Cash — No. 101

| Date | Explanation | Ref. | Debit | Credit | Balance |
|---|---|---|---|---|---|
| | | | | | |
| | | | | | |
| | | | | | |
| | | | | | |
| | | | | | |
| | | | | | |
| | | | | | |
| | | | | | |
| | | | | | |
| | | | | | |
| | | | | | |

Accounts Receivable — No. 112

| Date | Explanation | Ref. | Debit | Credit | Balance |
|---|---|---|---|---|---|
| | | | | | |
| | | | | | |

Land — No. 140

| Date | Explanation | Ref. | Debit | Credit | Balance |
|---|---|---|---|---|---|
| | | | | | |
| | | | | | |

Buildings — No. 145

| Date | Explanation | Ref. | Debit | Credit | Balance |
|---|---|---|---|---|---|
| | | | | | |
| | | | | | |

Equipment — No. 157

| Date | Explanation | Ref. | Debit | Credit | Balance |
|---|---|---|---|---|---|
| | | | | | |
| | | | | | |

Accounts Payable — No. 201

| Date | Explanation | Ref. | Debit | Credit | Balance |
|---|---|---|---|---|---|
| | | | | | |
| | | | | | |
| | | | | | |
| | | | | | |

Name | **Problem 2-5A Continued**
Section
Date | **Starlite Theater**

(a) and (c) (Continued)

L. Baroni, Capital — No. 301

| Date | Explanation | Ref. | Debit | Credit | Balance |
|---|---|---|---|---|---|
| | | | | | |
| | | | | | |

Admission Revenue — No. 405

| Date | Explanation | Ref. | Debit | Credit | Balance |
|---|---|---|---|---|---|
| | | | | | |
| | | | | | |
| | | | | | |
| | | | | | |

Concession Revenue — No. 406

| Date | Explanation | Ref. | Debit | Credit | Balance |
|---|---|---|---|---|---|
| | | | | | |
| | | | | | |

Advertising Expense — No. 610

| Date | Explanation | Ref. | Debit | Credit | Balance |
|---|---|---|---|---|---|
| | | | | | |
| | | | | | |
| | | | | | |

Film Rental Expense — No. 632

| Date | Explanation | Ref. | Debit | Credit | Balance |
|---|---|---|---|---|---|
| | | | | | |
| | | | | | |
| | | | | | |

Salaries Expense — No. 726

| Date | Explanation | Ref. | Debit | Credit | Balance |
|---|---|---|---|---|---|
| | | | | | |
| | | | | | |
| | | | | | |

Name
Section
Date

**Problem 2-5A Continued**

**Starlite Theater**

(b) General Journal J1

| Date | Account Titles and Explanation | Ref. | Debit | Credit |
|---|---|---|---|---|

 

(b) (Continued) General Journal J1

| Date | Account Titles and Explanation | Ref. | Debit | Credit |
|---|---|---|---|---|

(d)

STARLITE THEATER
Trial Balance
March 31, 1999

| | Debit | Credit |
|---|---|---|
| Cash | | |
| Accounts Receivable | | |
| Land | | |
| Equipment | | |
| Accounts Payable | | |
| L. Baroni, Capital | | |
| Admission Revenue | | |
| Concession Revenue | | |
| Advertising Expense | | |
| Film Rental Expense | | |
| Salaries Expense | | |

Name **Problem 2-1B**

Section

Date **Adventure Park**

General Journal J1

| Date | Account Titles and Explanation | Ref. | Debit | Credit |
|---|---|---|---|---|

 

Name **Problem 2-2B**

Section

Date **Lisa Heins, CPA**

11200
40
448000

(a) General Journal J1

| Date | Account Titles and Explanation | Ref. | Debit | Credit |
|---|---|---|---|---|
| May 1 | Cash | 101 | 32000 | |
| | Lisa Heins Capital | 301 | | 32000 |
| | Invest. Cash in Business | | | |
| | | | | |
| 3 | Supplies | 126 | 1200 | |
| | A/P | 201 | | 1200 |
| | | | | |
| 7 | Rent expense | 729 | 900 | |
| | Cash | 101 | | 900 |
| | | | | |
| 11 | A/R | 201 | 1100 | |
| | Service Rev | 400 | | 1100 |
| | | | | |
| 12 | Cash | 101 | 3500 | |
| | Unearned Rev. | 205 | | 3500 |
| | | | | |
| 17 | Cash | 101 | 1200 | |
| | Service Rev | 400 | | 1200 |
| | | | | |
| 31 | Salaries exp | 726 | 1000 | |
| | Cash | 101 | | 1000 |
| | | | | |
| 31 | A/P | 201 | 480 | |
| | Cash | 101 | | 480 |

Name

Section

Date

**Problem 2-2B Continued**

**Lisa Heins, CPA**

(b)

Cash — No. 101

| Date | Explanation | Ref. | Debit | Credit | Balance |
|---|---|---|---|---|---|
| | | | | | |
| | | | | | |
| | | | | | |
| | | | | | |
| | | | | | |
| | | | | | |
| | | | | | |

Accounts Receivable — No. 112

| Date | Explanation | Ref. | Debit | Credit | Balance |
|---|---|---|---|---|---|
| | | | | | |
| | | | | | |
| | | | | | |

Supplies — No. 126

| Date | Explanation | Ref. | Debit | Credit | Balance |
|---|---|---|---|---|---|
| | | | | | |
| | | | | | |
| | | | | | |

Accounts Payable — No. 201

| Date | Explanation | Ref. | Debit | Credit | Balance |
|---|---|---|---|---|---|
| | | | | | |
| | | | | | |
| | | | | | |
| | | | | | |

Unearned Revenue — No. 205

| Date | Explanation | Ref. | Debit | Credit | Balance |
|---|---|---|---|---|---|
| | | | | | |
| | | | | | |
| | | | | | |

Lisa Heins, Capital — No. 301

| Date | Explanation | Ref. | Debit | Credit | Balance |
|---|---|---|---|---|---|
| | | | | | |
| | | | | | |
| | | | | | |

(b) (Continued)

Service Revenue No. 400

| Date | Explanation | Ref. | Debit | Credit | Balance |
| --- | --- | --- | --- | --- | --- |
| | | | | | |
| | | | | | |
| | | | | | |

Salaries Expense No. 726

| Date | Explanation | Ref. | Debit | Credit | Balance |
| --- | --- | --- | --- | --- | --- |
| | | | | | |
| | | | | | |
| | | | | | |

Rent Expense No. 729

| Date | Explanation | Ref. | Debit | Credit | Balance |
| --- | --- | --- | --- | --- | --- |
| | | | | | |
| | | | | | |
| | | | | | |

(c)

LISA HEINS, CPA
Trial Balance
April 30, 1999

| | | Debit | Credit | |
| --- | --- | --- | --- | --- |
| 1 | Cash | | | 1 |
| 2 | Accounts Receivable | | | 2 |
| 3 | Supplies | | | 3 |
| 4 | Accounts Payable | | | 4 |
| 5 | Unearned Revenue | | | 5 |
| 6 | Lisa Heins, Capital | | | 6 |
| 7 | Service Revenue | | | 7 |
| 8 | Salaries Expense | | | 8 |
| 9 | Rent Expense | | | 9 |
| 10 | | | | 10 |
| 11 | | | | 11 |

Name
Section
Date

**Problem 2-3B**

**Steiner Dry Cleaners**

(a) and (c)

Cash — No. 101

| Date | Explanation | Ref. | Debit | Credit | Balance |
|---|---|---|---|---|---|
| | | | | | |
| | | | | | |
| | | | | | |
| | | | | | |
| | | | | | |
| | | | | | |
| | | | | | |
| | | | | | |

Accounts Receivable — No. 112

| Date | Explanation | Ref. | Debit | Credit | Balance |
|---|---|---|---|---|---|
| | | | | | |
| | | | | | |
| | | | | | |
| | | | | | |

Supplies — No. 126

| Date | Explanation | Ref. | Debit | Credit | Balance |
|---|---|---|---|---|---|
| | | | | | |
| | | | | | |
| | | | | | |

Equipment — No. 157

| Date | Explanation | Ref. | Debit | Credit | Balance |
|---|---|---|---|---|---|
| | | | | | |
| | | | | | |
| | | | | | |

Accounts Payable — No. 201

| Date | Explanation | Ref. | Debit | Credit | Balance |
|---|---|---|---|---|---|
| | | | | | |
| | | | | | |
| | | | | | |
| | | | | | |

Name **Problem 2-3B Continued**

Section

Date **Steiner Dry Cleaners**

(a) and (c) (Continued)

Unearned Revenue — No. 206

| Date | Explanation | Ref. | Debit | Credit | Balance |
|---|---|---|---|---|---|
| | | | | | |
| | | | | | |

C. Steiner, Capital — No. 301

| Date | Explanation | Ref. | Debit | Credit | Balance |
|---|---|---|---|---|---|
| | | | | | |
| | | | | | |

C. Steiner, Drawing — No. 306

| Date | Explanation | Ref. | Debit | Credit | Balance |
|---|---|---|---|---|---|
| | | | | | |
| | | | | | |

Dry Cleaning Revenue — No. 428

| Date | Explanation | Ref. | Debit | Credit | Balance |
|---|---|---|---|---|---|
| | | | | | |
| | | | | | |
| | | | | | |

Repair Expense — No. 622

| Date | Explanation | Ref. | Debit | Credit | Balance |
|---|---|---|---|---|---|
| | | | | | |
| | | | | | |

Salaries Expense — No. 726

| Date | Explanation | Ref. | Debit | Credit | Balance |
|---|---|---|---|---|---|
| | | | | | |
| | | | | | |
| | | | | | |

Utilities Expense — No. 732

| Date | Explanation | Ref. | Debit | Credit | Balance |
|---|---|---|---|---|---|
| | | | | | |
| | | | | | |

Name

Section

Date

**Problem 2-3B Continued**

**Steiner Dry Cleaners**

(b) General Journal J1

| | Date | Account Titles and Explanation | Ref. | Debit | Credit | |
|---|---|---|---|---|---|---|
| 1 | | | | | | 1 |
| 2 | | | | | | 2 |
| 3 | | | | | | 3 |
| 4 | | | | | | 4 |
| 5 | | | | | | 5 |
| 6 | | | | | | 6 |
| 7 | | | | | | 7 |
| 8 | | | | | | 8 |
| 9 | | | | | | 9 |
| 10 | | | | | | 10 |
| 11 | | | | | | 11 |
| 12 | | | | | | 12 |
| 13 | | | | | | 13 |
| 14 | | | | | | 14 |
| 15 | | | | | | 15 |
| 16 | | | | | | 16 |
| 17 | | | | | | 17 |
| 18 | | | | | | 18 |
| 19 | | | | | | 19 |
| 20 | | | | | | 20 |
| 21 | | | | | | 21 |
| 22 | | | | | | 22 |
| 23 | | | | | | 23 |
| 24 | | | | | | 24 |
| 25 | | | | | | 25 |
| 26 | | | | | | 26 |
| 27 | | | | | | 27 |
| 28 | | | | | | 28 |
| 29 | | | | | | 29 |
| 30 | | | | | | 30 |
| 31 | | | | | | 31 |
| 32 | | | | | | 32 |
| 33 | | | | | | 33 |
| 34 | | | | | | 34 |
| 35 | | | | | | 35 |
| 36 | | | | | | 36 |
| 37 | | | | | | 37 |
| 38 | | | | | | 38 |
| 39 | | | | | | 39 |
| 40 | | | | | | 40 |

(d)

STEINER DRY CLEANERS
Trial Balance
July 31, 1999

| | | Debit | Credit | |
|---|---|---|---|---|
| 1 | Cash | | | 1 |
| 2 | Accounts Receivable | | | 2 |
| 3 | Supplies | | | 3 |
| 4 | Equipment | | | 4 |
| 5 | Accounts Payable | | | 5 |
| 6 | Unearned Revenue | | | 6 |
| 7 | C. Steiner, Capital | | | 7 |
| 8 | C. Steiner, Drawing | | | 8 |
| 9 | Dry Cleaning Revenue | | | 9 |
| 10 | Salaries Expense | | | 10 |
| 11 | Utilities Expense | | | 11 |
| 12 | Repair Expense | | | 12 |
| 13 | | | | 13 |
| 14 | | | | 14 |
| 15 | | | | 15 |

Name

Section

Date

**Problem 2-4B**

**Shawnee Company**

SHAWNEE COMPANY

Trial Balance

May 31, 1999

| | Debit | Credit |
|---|---|---|
| | | |

Journal Entry Aids:

| | | |
|---|---|---|
| | | |

Name **Problem 2-5B**

Section

Date **Grand Theater**

(a) and (c)

Cash No. 101

| Date | Explanation | Ref. | Debit | Credit | Balance |
|---|---|---|---|---|---|
| | | | | | |
| | | | | | |
| | | | | | |
| | | | | | |
| | | | | | |
| | | | | | |
| | | | | | |
| | | | | | |
| | | | | | |
| | | | | | |

Accounts Receivable No. 112

| Date | Explanation | Ref. | Debit | Credit | Balance |
|---|---|---|---|---|---|
| | | | | | |
| | | | | | |

Prepaid Rentals No. 136

| Date | Explanation | Ref. | Debit | Credit | Balance |
|---|---|---|---|---|---|
| | | | | | |
| | | | | | |

Land No. 140

| Date | Explanation | Ref. | Debit | Credit | Balance |
|---|---|---|---|---|---|
| | | | | | |
| | | | | | |

Buildings No. 145

| Date | Explanation | Ref. | Debit | Credit | Balance |
|---|---|---|---|---|---|
| | | | | | |
| | | | | | |

Equipment No. 157

| Date | Explanation | Ref. | Debit | Credit | Balance |
|---|---|---|---|---|---|
| | | | | | |
| | | | | | |

Accounts Payable No. 201

| Date | Explanation | Ref. | Debit | Credit | Balance |
|---|---|---|---|---|---|
| | | | | | |
| | | | | | |
| | | | | | |
| | | | | | |

(a) and (c) (Continued)

Mortgage Payable No. 275

| Date | Explanation | Ref. | Debit | Credit | Balance |
|---|---|---|---|---|---|
| | | | | | |
| | | | | | |
| | | | | | |

Frances Hill, Capital No. 301

| Date | Explanation | Ref. | Debit | Credit | Balance |
|---|---|---|---|---|---|
| | | | | | |
| | | | | | |

Admission Revenue No. 405

| Date | Explanation | Ref. | Debit | Credit | Balance |
|---|---|---|---|---|---|
| | | | | | |
| | | | | | |
| | | | | | |

Concession Revenue No. 406

| Date | Explanation | Ref. | Debit | Credit | Balance |
|---|---|---|---|---|---|
| | | | | | |
| | | | | | |

Advertising Expense No. 610

| Date | Explanation | Ref. | Debit | Credit | Balance |
|---|---|---|---|---|---|
| | | | | | |
| | | | | | |

Film Rental Expense No. 632

| Date | Explanation | Ref. | Debit | Credit | Balance |
|---|---|---|---|---|---|
| | | | | | |
| | | | | | |
| | | | | | |

Salaries Expense No. 726

| Date | Explanation | Ref. | Debit | Credit | Balance |
|---|---|---|---|---|---|
| | | | | | |
| | | | | | |

 

Name

Section

Date

**Problem 2-5B Continued**

**Grand Theater**

(b) General Journal J1

| Date | Account Titles and Explanation | Ref. | Debit | Credit |
|---|---|---|---|---|

(b) (Continued) General Journal J1

| Date | Account Titles and Explanation | Ref. | Debit | Credit |
|---|---|---|---|---|
| | | | | |
| | | | | |
| | | | | |
| | | | | |
| | | | | |
| | | | | |
| | | | | |
| | | | | |
| | | | | |
| | | | | |
| | | | | |
| | | | | |
| | | | | |
| | | | | |

(d)

GRAND THEATER
Trial Balance
April 30, 1999

| | Debit | Credit |
|---|---|---|
| Cash | | |
| Accounts Receivable | | |
| Prepaid Rentals | | |
| Land | | |
| Buildings | | |
| Equipment | | |
| Accounts Payable | | |
| Mortgage Payable | | |
| Fran Holley, Capital | | |
| Admission Revenue | | |
| Concession Revenue | | |
| Advertising Expense | | |
| Film Rental Expense | | |
| Salaries Expense | | |
| | | |
| | | |
| | | |

 

Name

Section

Date

**Chapter 2 Financial Reporting Problem**

**Kellogg Company**

(a)

| Account | Side of Account for Increase | Side of Account for Decrease | Normal Balance |
|---|---|---|---|
| Accounts Payable | | | |
| | | | |
| Accounts Receivable | | | |
| | | | |
| Property | | | |
| | | | |
| Notes Payable | | | |
| | | | |
| Interest Expense | | | |
| | | | |
| Inventories | | | |
| | | | |

(b) and (c)

| | Accounts | Effect |
|---|---|---|
| (b) When | | |
| Accounts Receivable is decreased | | |
| | | |
| Accounts Payable is decreased | | |
| | | |
| Inventories are increased | | |
| | | |
| | | |
| | | |
| (c) When | | |
| Interest Expense is increased | | |
| | | |
| OR | | |
| | | |
| Property is increased | | |
| | | |
| OR | | |
| | | |
| | | |
| | | |

Name

Section

Date

**Chapter 2 Comparative Analysis Problem**

**Kellogg vs. General Mills**

(a) Kellogg

1.

2.

3.

4.

General Mills

1.

2.

3.

4.

(b)

Name

Section

Date

**Bob Evans Farms, Inc.**

(a)

(b)

(c)

Name

Section

Date

**Chapter 2 Group Decision Case**

**Daniels Riding Academy**

(a)

General Journal

| | Date | Account Titles and Explanation | Ref. | Debit | Credit | |
|---|---|---|---|---|---|---|
| 1 | | | | | | 1 |
| 2 | | | | | | 2 |
| 3 | | | | | | 3 |
| 4 | | | | | | 4 |
| 5 | | | | | | 5 |
| 6 | | | | | | 6 |
| 7 | | | | | | 7 |
| 8 | | | | | | 8 |
| 9 | | | | | | 9 |
| 10 | | | | | | 10 |
| 11 | | | | | | 11 |
| 12 | | | | | | 12 |
| 13 | | | | | | 13 |
| 14 | | | | | | 14 |
| 15 | | | | | | 15 |
| 16 | | | | | | 16 |
| 17 | | | | | | 17 |
| 18 | | | | | | 18 |
| 19 | | | | | | 19 |
| 20 | | | | | | 20 |
| 21 | | | | | | 21 |
| 22 | | | | | | 22 |
| 23 | | | | | | 23 |
| 24 | | | | | | 24 |
| 25 | | | | | | 25 |
| 26 | | | | | | 26 |
| 27 | | | | | | 27 |
| 28 | | | | | | 28 |
| 29 | | | | | | 29 |
| 30 | | | | | | 30 |
| 31 | | | | | | 31 |
| 32 | | | | | | 32 |
| 33 | | | | | | 33 |
| 34 | | | | | | 34 |
| 35 | | | | | | 35 |
| 36 | | | | | | 36 |
| 37 | | | | | | 37 |
| 38 | | | | | | 38 |
| 39 | | | | | | 39 |
| 40 | | | | | | 40 |

Name

Section

Date



(b)

(c) and (d)

| | |
|---|---|
| (c) Net income as reported | 4500 |
| (d) Cash as reported | 12475 |

Name _______________ **Chapter 2 Real-World Focus**

Section _______________

Date _______________ **Chapter 2 Ethics Case**

**REAL-WORLD FOCUS** — Automated Security Holdings

(a)

(b)

(c)

**ETHICS CASE** — Staples Company

(a)

(b)

(c)

Name

Section

Date

Name

Section

Date

Name

Section

Date

Name

Section

Date

Name

Section

Date



#1

| Adj. | (a) Type of Adjustment | (b) Account Relationship | (c) Accounts before Adjustment |
|---|---|---|---|
| | | | |
| 1. | | | |
| | | | |
| | | | |
| 2. | | | |
| | | | |
| | | | |
| 3. | | | |
| | | | |
| | | | |
| 4. | | | |
| | | | |
| | | | |
| 5. | | | |
| | | | |
| | | | |
| 6. | | | |
| | | | |
| | | | |

#2 General Journal

| Date | Account Titles and Explanation | Ref. | Debit | Credit |
|---|---|---|---|---|
| mach 31 | Depreciation exp | | 750 | |
| | Accum Dep | | | 750 |
| | | | | |
| March 31 | Unearned Rent Rev. | | 3100 | |
| | Rent Rev. | | | 3100 |
| | | | | |
| March 31 | ~~Interest Payable~~ Intn exp. | | 500 | |
| | ~~NOTES Payable~~ Intrns Pay | | | 500 |
| | | | | |
| | Supples exp | | 1950 | |
| | Supplies | | | 1950 |
| | | | | |
| | Ins exp | | 940 | |
| | Prepd ins | | | 940 |
| | | | | |
| | | | | |

Name

Section

Date



General Journal

| Date | Account Titles and Explanation | Debit | Credit |
|---|---|---|---|
| **#3** | | | |
| **#4** | | | |

Name

Section

Date



**#5**

**#6**

Name

Section

Date

**Exercises 3-7 to 3-8**

General Journal

| Date | Account Titles and Explanations | Debit | Credit |
|---|---|---|---|
| **#7** | | | |
| **#8** | | | |

Name **Exercise 3-9**

Section

Date **Lund Company**

LUND COMPANY
Income Statement
For the Year Ended August 31, 1999

LUND COMPANY
Owner's Equity Statement
For the Year Ended August 31, 1999

LUND COMPANY
Balance Sheet
August 31, 1999

Name

Section

Date

**Exercise 3-1**

**Cash vs. Accrua**

(a)

(b)

(c)

Name

Section

Date

***Exercise 3-11**

**Harmony Company**

(a)

CASH

SERVICE REVENUE

INSURANCE EXPENSE

SUPPLIES EXPENSE

(b)

PREPAID INSURANCE

INSURANCE EXPENSE

SUPPLIES

SUPPLIES EXPENSE

UNEARNED REVENUE

SERVICE REVENUE

(c)

Name **Problem 3-1A**

Section

Date **Midwest Tours**

(a) General Journal J2

| Date | Account Titles and Explanation | Ref. | Debit | Credit |
|---|---|---|---|---|

 

Name Problem 3-1A Continued

Section

Date Midwest Tours

(b)

Cash

| Date | Explanation | Ref. | Debit | Credit | Balance |
|---|---|---|---|---|---|
| | | | | | |
| | | | | | |

Accounts Receivable

| Date | Explanation | Ref. | Debit | Credit | Balance |
|---|---|---|---|---|---|
| | | | | | |
| | | | | | |
| | | | | | |

Prepaid Insurance

| Date | Explanation | Ref. | Debit | Credit | Balance |
|---|---|---|---|---|---|
| | | | | | |
| | | | | | |
| | | | | | |

Office Equipment

| Date | Explanation | Ref. | Debit | Credit | Balance |
|---|---|---|---|---|---|
| | | | | | |
| | | | | | |

Accumulated Depreciation — Office Equipment

| Date | Explanation | Ref. | Debit | Credit | Balance |
|---|---|---|---|---|---|
| | | | | | |
| | | | | | |
| | | | | | |

Buses

| Date | Explanation | Ref. | Debit | Credit | Balance |
|---|---|---|---|---|---|
| | | | | | |
| | | | | | |

Accumulated Depreciation — Buses

| Date | Explanation | Ref. | Debit | Credit | Balance |
|---|---|---|---|---|---|
| | | | | | |
| | | | | | |
| | | | | | |

(b) (Continued)

Salaries Payable

| Date | Explanation | Ref. | Debit | Credit | Balance |
| --- | --- | --- | --- | --- | --- |
| | | | | | |
| | | | | | |

Interest Payable

| Date | Explanation | Ref. | Debit | Credit | Balance |
| --- | --- | --- | --- | --- | --- |
| | | | | | |
| | | | | | |

Notes Payable

| Date | Explanation | Ref. | Debit | Credit | Balance |
| --- | --- | --- | --- | --- | --- |
| | | | | | |
| | | | | | |

Unearned Tour Revenue

| Date | Explanation | Ref. | Debit | Credit | Balance |
| --- | --- | --- | --- | --- | --- |
| | | | | | |
| | | | | | |
| | | | | | |

Alan Kinsley, Capital

| Date | Explanation | Ref. | Debit | Credit | Balance |
| --- | --- | --- | --- | --- | --- |
| | | | | | |
| | | | | | |

Tour Revenue

| Date | Explanation | Ref. | Debit | Credit | Balance |
| --- | --- | --- | --- | --- | --- |
| | | | | | |
| | | | | | |
| | | | | | |
| | | | | | |

Salaries Expense

| Date | Explanation | Ref. | Debit | Credit | Balance |
| --- | --- | --- | --- | --- | --- |
| | | | | | |
| | | | | | |
| | | | | | |

**Problem 3-1A Continued**

**Midwest Tours**

(b) (Continued)

Advertising Expense

| Date | Explanation | Ref. | Debit | Credit | Balance |
|---|---|---|---|---|---|
| | | | | | |
| | | | | | |

Gas and Oil Expense

| Date | Explanation | Ref. | Debit | Credit | Balance |
|---|---|---|---|---|---|
| | | | | | |
| | | | | | |

Insurance Expense

| Date | Explanation | Ref. | Debit | Credit | Balance |
|---|---|---|---|---|---|
| | | | | | |
| | | | | | |

Depreciation Expense — Office Equipment

| Date | Explanation | Ref. | Debit | Credit | Balance |
|---|---|---|---|---|---|
| | | | | | |
| | | | | | |

Depreciation Expense — Buses

| Date | Explanation | Ref. | Debit | Credit | Balance |
|---|---|---|---|---|---|
| | | | | | |
| | | | | | |

Interest Expense

| Date | Explanation | Ref. | Debit | Credit | Balance |
|---|---|---|---|---|---|
| | | | | | |
| | | | | | |

(c)

MIDWEST TOURS
Adjusted Trial Balance
June 30, 1999

| | Debit | Credit |
|---|---|---|

Name

Section

Date

**Problem 3-2A**

**Super Motel**

(a) General Journal J1

| Date | Account Titles and Explanation | Ref. | Debit | Credit |
|---|---|---|---|---|
| | | | | |

(b)

Cash

| Date | Explanation | Ref. | Debit | Credit | Balance |
|---|---|---|---|---|---|
| | | | | | |
| | | | | | |

Prepaid Insurance

| Date | Explanation | Ref. | Debit | Credit | Balance |
|---|---|---|---|---|---|
| | | | | | |
| | | | | | |
| | | | | | |

Supplies

| Date | Explanation | Ref. | Debit | Credit | Balance |
|---|---|---|---|---|---|
| | | | | | |
| | | | | | |
| | | | | | |

Land

| Date | Explanation | Ref. | Debit | Credit | Balance |
|---|---|---|---|---|---|
| | | | | | |
| | | | | | |

Lodge

| Date | Explanation | Ref. | Debit | Credit | Balance |
|---|---|---|---|---|---|
| | | | | | |
| | | | | | |

Accumulated Depreciation — Lodge

| Date | Explanation | Ref. | Debit | Credit | Balance |
|---|---|---|---|---|---|
| | | | | | |
| | | | | | |

Furniture

| Date | Explanation | Ref. | Debit | Credit | Balance |
|---|---|---|---|---|---|
| | | | | | |
| | | | | | |

(b) (Continued)

Accumulated Depreciation — Furniture

| Date | Explanation | Ref. | Debit | Credit | Balance |
|---|---|---|---|---|---|
| | | | | | |
| | | | | | |

Accounts Payable

| Date | Explanation | Ref. | Debit | Credit | Balance |
|---|---|---|---|---|---|
| | | | | | |
| | | | | | |

Unearned Rent Revenue

| Date | Explanation | Ref. | Debit | Credit | Balance |
|---|---|---|---|---|---|
| | | | | | |
| | | | | | |
| | | | | | |

Salaries Payable

| Date | Explanation | Ref. | Debit | Credit | Balance |
|---|---|---|---|---|---|
| | | | | | |
| | | | | | |

Interest Payable

| Date | Explanation | Ref. | Debit | Credit | Balance |
|---|---|---|---|---|---|
| | | | | | |
| | | | | | |

Mortgage Payable

| Date | Explanation | Ref. | Debit | Credit | Balance |
|---|---|---|---|---|---|
| | | | | | |
| | | | | | |

Sara Sulton, Capital

| Date | Explanation | Ref. | Debit | Credit | Balance |
|---|---|---|---|---|---|
| | | | | | |
| | | | | | |

(b) (Continued)

Rent Revenue

| Date | Explanation | Ref. | Debit | Credit | Balance |
|---|---|---|---|---|---|
| | | | | | |
| | | | | | |
| | | | | | |

Salaries Expense

| Date | Explanation | Ref. | Debit | Credit | Balance |
|---|---|---|---|---|---|
| | | | | | |
| | | | | | |
| | | | | | |

Utilities Expense

| Date | Explanation | Ref. | Debit | Credit | Balance |
|---|---|---|---|---|---|
| | | | | | |
| | | | | | |

Advertising Expense

| Date | Explanation | Ref. | Debit | Credit | Balance |
|---|---|---|---|---|---|
| | | | | | |
| | | | | | |

Interest Expense

| Date | Explanation | Ref. | Debit | Credit | Balance |
|---|---|---|---|---|---|
| | | | | | |
| | | | | | |

Insurance Expense

| Date | Explanation | Ref. | Debit | Credit | Balance |
|---|---|---|---|---|---|
| | | | | | |
| | | | | | |

Supplies Expense

| Date | Explanation | Ref. | Debit | Credit | Balance |
|---|---|---|---|---|---|
| | | | | | |
| | | | | | |

Name

Section

Date



(b) (Continued)

Depreciation Expense — Lodge

| Date | Explanation | Ref. | Debit | Credit | Balance |
| --- | --- | --- | --- | --- | --- |
| | | | | | |
| | | | | | |

Depreciation Expense — Furniture

| Date | Explanation | Ref. | Debit | Credit | Balance |
| --- | --- | --- | --- | --- | --- |
| | | | | | |
| | | | | | |

(c)

SUPER MOTEL
Adjusted Trial Balance
May 31, 1999

| | | Debit | Credit | |
| --- | --- | --- | --- | --- |
| 1 | | | | 1 |
| 2 | | | | 2 |
| 3 | | | | 3 |
| 4 | | | | 4 |
| 5 | | | | 5 |
| 6 | | | | 6 |
| 7 | | | | 7 |
| 8 | | | | 8 |
| 9 | | | | 9 |
| 10 | | | | 10 |
| 11 | | | | 11 |
| 12 | | | | 12 |
| 13 | | | | 13 |
| 14 | | | | 14 |
| 15 | | | | 15 |
| 16 | | | | 16 |
| 17 | | | | 17 |
| 18 | | | | 18 |
| 19 | | | | 19 |
| 20 | | | | 20 |
| 21 | | | | 21 |
| 22 | | | | 22 |
| 23 | | | | 23 |
| 24 | | | | 24 |
| 25 | | | | 25 |
| 26 | | | | 26 |

(d)

SUPER MOTEL
Income Statement
For the Month Ended May 31, 1999

SUPER MOTEL
Owner's Equity Statement
For the Month Ended May 31, 1999

Name

Section

Date

**Problem 3-2A Concluded**

**Super Motel**

(d) (Continued)

SUPER MOTEL

Balance Sheet

May 31, 1999

Assets

Liabilities and Owner's Equity

Name

Section

Date

**Problem 3-3A**

**Irabu Co.**

(a)

General Journal

| Date | Account Titles and Explanation | Ref. | Debit | Credit |
|---|---|---|---|---|
| | | | | |

(b)

IRABU CO.
Income Statement
For the Quarter Ended September 30, 1999

| | | | |
|---|---|---|---|
| Commis Rev | | | 14600 |
| Rent Rev | | | 700 |
| Total Rev. | | | 15300 |
| Expeses | | | |
| Saleries Exp | | 9400 | |
| Rent Exp | | 1500 | |
| Dep Exp | | 350 | |
| Supplies Exp | | 200 | |
| Utilities Exp | | 510 | |
| Interest Exp | | 50 | |
| Total Exp | 12010 | | |
| | | | |
| | | | |
| Net Income | | | 3290 |

(b) (Continued)

IRABU CO.
Owner's Equity Statement
For the Quarter Ended September 30, 1999

| | | |
|---|---|---|
| IRAbu Cap JULY 1 1999 | 14000 — | |
| Net Income | 3290 | |
| | 17290 | |
| Less DRAWING | 600 | |
| | | |
| IRAbu CApt. | 16690 | |
| | | |

IRABU CO.
Balance Sheet
September 30, 1999

| | | |
|---|---|---|
| **Assets** | | |
| CASh | | 6700 |
| A/R | | 1000 |
| Pre-Pd Rent | | 900 |
| Supplies | | 1000 |
| Equipment | 15000 | |
| Less Acum Dep. | 350 | 14650 |
| | | |
| Total ASSETS | | 24250 |
| **Liabilities and Owner's Equity** | | |
| NOTES Payable | | 5000 |
| A/P | | 1510 |
| SAlary Pay | | 400 |
| Intrest Pay | | 50 |
| Unearned Rent Rev | | 600 |
| Total Liabilities | | 7560 |
| | | |
| | | |
| | | |
| IRAbu Cap. Sept 30, 1999 | | 16690 |

(c)

Name

Section

Date

**Problem 3-4A**

**Davis Company**

General Journal

| | Date | Account Titles and Explanation | Ref. | Debit | Credit | |
|---|---|---|---|---|---|---|
| 1 | | | | | | 1 |
| 2 | | | | | | 2 |
| 3 | | | | | | 3 |
| 4 | | | | | | 4 |
| 5 | | | | | | 5 |
| 6 | | | | | | 6 |
| 7 | | | | | | 7 |
| 8 | | | | | | 8 |
| 9 | | | | | | 9 |
| 10 | | | | | | 10 |
| 11 | | | | | | 11 |
| 12 | | | | | | 12 |
| 13 | | | | | | 13 |
| 14 | | | | | | 14 |
| 15 | | | | | | 15 |
| 16 | | | | | | 16 |
| 17 | | | | | | 17 |
| 18 | | | | | | 18 |
| 19 | | | | | | 19 |
| 20 | | | | | | 20 |
| 21 | | | | | | 21 |
| 22 | | | | | | 22 |
| 23 | | | | | | 23 |
| 24 | | | | | | 24 |
| 25 | | | | | | 25 |
| 26 | | | | | | 26 |
| 27 | | | | | | 27 |
| 28 | | | | | | 28 |
| 29 | | | | | | 29 |
| 30 | | | | | | 30 |
| 31 | | | | | | 31 |
| 32 | | | | | | 32 |
| 33 | | | | | | 33 |
| 34 | | | | | | 34 |
| 35 | | | | | | 35 |
| 36 | | | | | | 36 |
| 37 | | | | | | 37 |
| 38 | | | | | | 38 |
| 39 | | | | | | 39 |
| 40 | | | | | | 40 |

Name

Section

Date

**Problem 3-5A**

**Delino Equipment Repair**

(a), (c) and (e)

Cash — No. 101

| Date | Explanation | Ref. | Debit | Credit | Balance |
|---|---|---|---|---|---|
| | | | | | |
| | | | | | |
| | | | | | |
| | | | | | |
| | | | | | |
| | | | | | |
| | | | | | |
| | | | | | |
| | | | | | |

Accounts Receivable — No. 112

| Date | Explanation | Ref. | Debit | Credit | Balance |
|---|---|---|---|---|---|
| | | | | | |
| | | | | | |
| | | | | | |
| | | | | | |

Supplies — No. 126

| Date | Explanation | Ref. | Debit | Credit | Balance |
|---|---|---|---|---|---|
| | | | | | |
| | | | | | |
| | | | | | |
| | | | | | |

Store Equipment — No. 153

| Date | Explanation | Ref. | Debit | Credit | Balance |
|---|---|---|---|---|---|
| | | | | | |
| | | | | | |
| | | | | | |

Accumulated Depreciation — Store Equipment — No. 154

| Date | Explanation | Ref. | Debit | Credit | Balance |
|---|---|---|---|---|---|
| | | | | | |
| | | | | | |
| | | | | | |

Name
Section
Date

**Problem 3-5A Continued**

**Delino Equipment Repair**

(a), (c) and (e) (Continued)

Accounts Payable — No. 201

| Date | Explanation | Ref. | Debit | Credit | Balance |
|---|---|---|---|---|---|
| | | | | | |
| | | | | | |
| | | | | | |
| | | | | | |
| | | | | | |

Unearned Service Revenue — No. 209

| Date | Explanation | Ref. | Debit | Credit | Balance |
|---|---|---|---|---|---|
| | | | | | |
| | | | | | |
| | | | | | |
| | | | | | |

Salaries Payable — No. 212

| Date | Explanation | Ref. | Debit | Credit | Balance |
|---|---|---|---|---|---|
| | | | | | |
| | | | | | |
| | | | | | |
| | | | | | |

P. Delino, Capital — No. 301

| Date | Explanation | Ref. | Debit | Credit | Balance |
|---|---|---|---|---|---|
| | | | | | |
| | | | | | |

Service Revenue — No. 407

| Date | Explanation | Ref. | Debit | Credit | Balance |
|---|---|---|---|---|---|
| | | | | | |
| | | | | | |
| | | | | | |
| | | | | | |

Depreciation Expense — No. 615

| Date | Explanation | Ref. | Debit | Credit | Balance |
|---|---|---|---|---|---|
| | | | | | |
| | | | | | |

 

Name

Section

Date

**Problem 3-5A Continued**

**Delino Equipment Repair**

(a), (c) and (e) (Continued)

Supplies Expense — No. 631

| Date | Explanation | Ref. | Debit | Credit | Balance |
|---|---|---|---|---|---|
| | | | | | |
| | | | | | |
| | | | | | |

Salaries Expense — No. 726

| Date | Explanation | Ref. | Debit | Credit | Balance |
|---|---|---|---|---|---|
| | | | | | |
| | | | | | |
| | | | | | |
| | | | | | |

Rent Expense — No. 729

| Date | Explanation | Ref. | Debit | Credit | Balance |
|---|---|---|---|---|---|
| | | | | | |
| | | | | | |

(b)

General Journal — J1

| Date | Account Titles and Explanation | Ref. | Debit | Credit |
|---|---|---|---|---|
| | | | | |
| | | | | |
| | | | | |
| | | | | |
| | | | | |
| | | | | |
| | | | | |
| | | | | |
| | | | | |
| | | | | |
| | | | | |
| | | | | |
| | | | | |
| | | | | |
| | | | | |
| | | | | |
| | | | | |
| | | | | |
| | | | | |
| | | | | |

(b) (Continued) General Journal J1

| Date | Account Titles and Explanation | Ref. | Debit | Credit |
|---|---|---|---|---|

(e) General Journal J2

| Date | Account Titles and Explanation | Ref. | Debit | Credit |
|---|---|---|---|---|

(d) and (f)

DELINO EQUIPMENT REPAIR
Trial Balances
November 30, 1999

| | Before Adjustment | | After Adjustment | |
|---|---|---|---|---|
| | Dr. | Cr. | Dr. | Cr. |
| | | | | |

(g)

DELINO EQUIPMENT REPAIR
Income Statement
For the Month Ended November 30, 1999

| | | |
|---|---|---|
| | | |

(g) (Continued)

DELINO EQUIPMENT REPAIR
Owner's Equity Statement
For the Month Ended November 30, 1999

DELINO EQUIPMENT REPAIR
Balance Sheet
November 30, 1999

Assets

Liabilities and Owner's Equity

Name

Section

Date

***Problem 3-6A**

**Cordero Graphics Company**

(a) General Journal

| Date | Account Titles and Explanation | Ref. | Debit | Credit |
|---|---|---|---|---|

(b)

CORDERO GRAPHICS COMPANY
Adjusted Trial Balance
June 30, 1999

| | Debit | Credit |
|---|---|---|

(c)

CORDERO GRAPHICS COMPANY
Income Statement
For the Six Months Ended June 30, 1999

Name

Section

Date

***Problem 3-6A Concluded**

**Cordero Graphics Company**

(c) (Continued)

CORDERO GRAPHICS COMPANY

Owner's Equity Statement

For the Six Months Ended June 30, 1999

CORDERO GRAPHICS COMPANY

Balance Sheet

June 30, 1999

Assets

Liabilities and Owner's Equity

Name

Section

Date

**Problem 3-1B**

**Orosco Security Service**

(a) General Journal J15

| Date | Account Titles and Explanation | Ref. | Debit | Credit |
|---|---|---|---|---|

Name
Section
Date

**Problem 3-1B Continued**

**Orosco Security Service**

(b)

Cash

| Date | Explanation | Ref. | Debit | Credit | Balance |
| --- | --- | --- | --- | --- | --- |
| | | | | | |
| | | | | | |

Accounts Receivable

| Date | Explanation | Ref. | Debit | Credit | Balance |
| --- | --- | --- | --- | --- | --- |
| | | | | | |
| | | | | | |
| | | | | | |

Prepaid Insurance

| Date | Explanation | Ref. | Debit | Credit | Balance |
| --- | --- | --- | --- | --- | --- |
| | | | | | |
| | | | | | |
| | | | | | |

Automobiles

| Date | Explanation | Ref. | Debit | Credit | Balance |
| --- | --- | --- | --- | --- | --- |
| | | | | | |
| | | | | | |

Accumulated Depreciation — Automobiles

| Date | Explanation | Ref. | Debit | Credit | Balance |
| --- | --- | --- | --- | --- | --- |
| | | | | | |
| | | | | | |

Notes Payable

| Date | Explanation | Ref. | Debit | Credit | Balance |
| --- | --- | --- | --- | --- | --- |
| | | | | | |
| | | | | | |

Accounts Payable

| Date | Explanation | Ref. | Debit | Credit | Balance |
| --- | --- | --- | --- | --- | --- |
| | | | | | |
| | | | | | |

(b) (Continued)

Interest Payable

| Date | Explanation | Ref. | Debit | Credit | Balance |
| --- | --- | --- | --- | --- | --- |
| | | | | | |
| | | | | | |

Salaries Payable

| Date | Explanation | Ref. | Debit | Credit | Balance |
| --- | --- | --- | --- | --- | --- |
| | | | | | |
| | | | | | |

Unearned Revenue

| Date | Explanation | Ref. | Debit | Credit | Balance |
| --- | --- | --- | --- | --- | --- |
| | | | | | |
| | | | | | |
| | | | | | |

C. Orosco, Capital

| Date | Explanation | Ref. | Debit | Credit | Balance |
| --- | --- | --- | --- | --- | --- |
| | | | | | |
| | | | | | |

Service Revenue

| Date | Explanation | Ref. | Debit | Credit | Balance |
| --- | --- | --- | --- | --- | --- |
| | | | | | |
| | | | | | |
| | | | | | |
| | | | | | |

Salaries Expense

| Date | Explanation | Ref. | Debit | Credit | Balance |
| --- | --- | --- | --- | --- | --- |
| | | | | | |
| | | | | | |
| | | | | | |

 

b) (Continued)

Repair Expense

| Date | Explanation | Ref. | Debit | Credit | Balance |
|---|---|---|---|---|---|
| | | | | | |
| | | | | | |
| | | | | | |

Gas and Oil Expense

| Date | Explanation | Ref. | Debit | Credit | Balance |
|---|---|---|---|---|---|
| | | | | | |
| | | | | | |
| | | | | | |

Insurance Expense

| Date | Explanation | Ref. | Debit | Credit | Balance |
|---|---|---|---|---|---|
| | | | | | |
| | | | | | |
| | | | | | |

Depreciation Expense — Automobiles

| Date | Explanation | Ref. | Debit | Credit | Balance |
|---|---|---|---|---|---|
| | | | | | |
| | | | | | |
| | | | | | |

Interest Expense

| Date | Explanation | Ref. | Debit | Credit | Balance |
|---|---|---|---|---|---|
| | | | | | |
| | | | | | |
| | | | | | |

(c)

OROSCO SECURITY SERVICE
Adjusted Trial Balance
December 31, 1999

| | Debit | Credit |
|---|---|---|

Name

Section

Date

**Problem 3-2B**

**Spring River Resort**

(a)

General Journal

| Date | Account Titles and Explanation | Ref. | Debit | Credit |
|---|---|---|---|---|

(b) Cash

| Date | Explanation | Ref. | Debit | Credit | Balance |
| --- | --- | --- | --- | --- | --- |
| | | | | | |
| | | | | | |

Accounts Receivable

| Date | Explanation | Ref. | Debit | Credit | Balance |
| --- | --- | --- | --- | --- | --- |
| | | | | | |
| | | | | | |

Prepaid Insurance

| Date | Explanation | Ref. | Debit | Credit | Balance |
| --- | --- | --- | --- | --- | --- |
| | | | | | |
| | | | | | |
| | | | | | |

Supplies

| Date | Explanation | Ref. | Debit | Credit | Balance |
| --- | --- | --- | --- | --- | --- |
| | | | | | |
| | | | | | |
| | | | | | |

Land

| Date | Explanation | Ref. | Debit | Credit | Balance |
| --- | --- | --- | --- | --- | --- |
| | | | | | |
| | | | | | |

Cottages

| Date | Explanation | Ref. | Debit | Credit | Balance |
| --- | --- | --- | --- | --- | --- |
| | | | | | |
| | | | | | |

Accumulated Depreciation — Cottages

| Date | Explanation | Ref. | Debit | Credit | Balance |
| --- | --- | --- | --- | --- | --- |
| | | | | | |
| | | | | | |

 

Name
Section
Date

Problem 3-2B Continued

Spring River Resort

(b) (Continued)

Furniture

| Date | Explanation | Ref. | Debit | Credit | Balance |
|---|---|---|---|---|---|
| | | | | | |
| | | | | | |

Accumulated Depreciation — Furniture

| Date | Explanation | Ref. | Debit | Credit | Balance |
|---|---|---|---|---|---|
| | | | | | |
| | | | | | |

Accounts Payable

| Date | Explanation | Ref. | Debit | Credit | Balance |
|---|---|---|---|---|---|
| | | | | | |
| | | | | | |

Unearned Rent Revenue

| Date | Explanation | Ref. | Debit | Credit | Balance |
|---|---|---|---|---|---|
| | | | | | |
| | | | | | |
| | | | | | |

Salaries Payable

| Date | Explanation | Ref. | Debit | Credit | Balance |
|---|---|---|---|---|---|
| | | | | | |
| | | | | | |

Interest Payable

| Date | Explanation | Ref. | Debit | Credit | Balance |
|---|---|---|---|---|---|
| | | | | | |
| | | | | | |

Mortgage Payable

| Date | Explanation | Ref. | Debit | Credit | Balance |
|---|---|---|---|---|---|
| | | | | | |
| | | | | | |

Name | **Problem 3-2B Continue**
Section
Date | **Spring River Reso**

(b) (Continued)

P. Villone, Capital

| Date | Explanation | Ref. | Debit | Credit | Balance |
| --- | --- | --- | --- | --- | --- |
| | | | | | |
| | | | | | |

P. Villone, Drawing

| Date | Explanation | Ref. | Debit | Credit | Balance |
| --- | --- | --- | --- | --- | --- |
| | | | | | |
| | | | | | |

Rent Revenue

| Date | Explanation | Ref. | Debit | Credit | Balance |
| --- | --- | --- | --- | --- | --- |
| | | | | | |
| | | | | | |
| | | | | | |
| | | | | | |

Salaries Expense

| Date | Explanation | Ref. | Debit | Credit | Balance |
| --- | --- | --- | --- | --- | --- |
| | | | | | |
| | | | | | |
| | | | | | |

Utilities Expense

| Date | Explanation | Ref. | Debit | Credit | Balance |
| --- | --- | --- | --- | --- | --- |
| | | | | | |
| | | | | | |

Repair Expense

| Date | Explanation | Ref. | Debit | Credit | Balance |
| --- | --- | --- | --- | --- | --- |
| | | | | | |
| | | | | | |

Insurance Expense

| Date | Explanation | Ref. | Debit | Credit | Balance |
| --- | --- | --- | --- | --- | --- |
| | | | | | |
| | | | | | |

(b) (Continued)

Supplies Expense

| Date | Explanation | Ref. | Debit | Credit | Balance |
|---|---|---|---|---|---|
| | | | | | |
| | | | | | |

Depreciation Expense — Cottages

| Date | Explanation | Ref. | Debit | Credit | Balance |
|---|---|---|---|---|---|
| | | | | | |
| | | | | | |

Depreciation Expense — Furniture

| Date | Explanation | Ref. | Debit | Credit | Balance |
|---|---|---|---|---|---|
| | | | | | |
| | | | | | |

Interest Expense

| Date | Explanation | Ref. | Debit | Credit | Balance |
|---|---|---|---|---|---|
| | | | | | |
| | | | | | |

(c)

SPRING RIVER RESORT
Adjusted Trial Balance
August 31, 1999

| | Debit | Credit |
|---|---|---|
| | | |

 

Name

Section

Date

**Problem 3-2B Continued**

**Spring River Resort**

(d)

SPRING RIVER RESORT

Income Statement

For the Three Months Ended August 31, 1999

SPRING RIVER RESORT

Owner's Equity Statement

For the Three Months Ended August 31, 1999

(d) (Continued)

SPRING RIVER RESORT
Balance Sheet
August 31, 1999

| | | |
|---|---|---|
| Assets | | |
| Liabilities and Owner's Equity | | |

 

Name
Section
Date

**Problem 3-3B**

**Yount Advertising Agency**

(a)

General Journal

| Date | Account Titles and Explanation | Ref. | Debit | Credit |
| --- | --- | --- | --- | --- |

(b)

YOUNT ADVERTISING AGENCY
Income Statement
For the Year Ended December 31, 1999

(b) (Continued)

YOUNT ADVERTISING AGENCY
Owner's Equity Statement
For the Year Ended December 31, 1999

YOUNT ADVERTISING AGENCY
Balance Sheet
December 31, 1999

Assets

Liabilities and Owner's Equity

(c)

(1)

(2)

Name Problem 3-4B

Section

Date Oklahoma Company

General Journal

| | Date | Account Titles and Explanation | Ref. | Debit | Credit | |
|---|---|---|---|---|---|---|
| 1 | | | | | | 1 |
| 2 | | | | | | 2 |
| 3 | | | | | | 3 |
| 4 | | | | | | 4 |
| 5 | | | | | | 5 |
| 6 | | | | | | 6 |
| 7 | | | | | | 7 |
| 8 | | | | | | 8 |
| 9 | | | | | | 9 |
| 10 | | | | | | 10 |
| 11 | | | | | | 11 |
| 12 | | | | | | 12 |
| 13 | | | | | | 13 |
| 14 | | | | | | 14 |
| 15 | | | | | | 15 |
| 16 | | | | | | 16 |
| 17 | | | | | | 17 |
| 18 | | | | | | 18 |
| 19 | | | | | | 19 |
| 20 | | | | | | 20 |
| 21 | | | | | | 21 |
| 22 | | | | | | 22 |
| 23 | | | | | | 23 |
| 24 | | | | | | 24 |
| 25 | | | | | | 25 |
| 26 | | | | | | 26 |
| 27 | | | | | | 27 |
| 28 | | | | | | 28 |
| 29 | | | | | | 29 |
| 30 | | | | | | 30 |
| 31 | | | | | | 31 |
| 32 | | | | | | 32 |
| 33 | | | | | | 33 |
| 34 | | | | | | 34 |
| 35 | | | | | | 35 |
| 36 | | | | | | 36 |
| 37 | | | | | | 37 |
| 38 | | | | | | 38 |
| 39 | | | | | | 39 |
| 40 | | | | | | 40 |

Name

Section

Date

**Problem 3-5B**

**Silva Equipment Repair**

(a), (c) and (e)

Cash — No. 101

| Date | Explanation | Ref. | Debit | Credit | Balance |
|---|---|---|---|---|---|
| | | | | | |
| | | | | | |
| | | | | | |
| | | | | | |
| | | | | | |
| | | | | | |
| | | | | | |
| | | | | | |
| | | | | | |

Accounts Receivable — No. 112

| Date | Explanation | Ref. | Debit | Credit | Balance |
|---|---|---|---|---|---|
| | | | | | |
| | | | | | |
| | | | | | |
| | | | | | |

Supplies — No. 126

| Date | Explanation | Ref. | Debit | Credit | Balance |
|---|---|---|---|---|---|
| | | | | | |
| | | | | | |
| | | | | | |
| | | | | | |

Store Equipment — No. 153

| Date | Explanation | Ref. | Debit | Credit | Balance |
|---|---|---|---|---|---|
| | | | | | |
| | | | | | |
| | | | | | |

Accumulated Depreciation – Store Equipment — No. 154

| Date | Explanation | Ref. | Debit | Credit | Balance |
|---|---|---|---|---|---|
| | | | | | |
| | | | | | |
| | | | | | |

Name

Section

Date

**Problem 3-5B Continued**

**Silva Equipment Repair**

(a), (c) and (e) (Continued)

Accounts Payable — No. 201

| Date | Explanation | Ref. | Debit | Credit | Balance |
|---|---|---|---|---|---|
| | | | | | |
| | | | | | |
| | | | | | |
| | | | | | |
| | | | | | |

Unearned Service Revenue — No. 209

| Date | Explanation | Ref. | Debit | Credit | Balance |
|---|---|---|---|---|---|
| | | | | | |
| | | | | | |
| | | | | | |
| | | | | | |

Salaries Payable — No. 212

| Date | Explanation | Ref. | Debit | Credit | Balance |
|---|---|---|---|---|---|
| | | | | | |
| | | | | | |
| | | | | | |
| | | | | | |

J. Silva, Capital — No. 301

| Date | Explanation | Ref. | Debit | Credit | Balance |
|---|---|---|---|---|---|
| | | | | | |
| | | | | | |

Service Revenue — No. 407

| Date | Explanation | Ref. | Debit | Credit | Balance |
|---|---|---|---|---|---|
| | | | | | |
| | | | | | |
| | | | | | |
| | | | | | |

Depreciation Expense — No. 615

| Date | Explanation | Ref. | Debit | Credit | Balance |
|---|---|---|---|---|---|
| | | | | | |
| | | | | | |

Name

Section

Date

**Problem 3-5B Continued**

**Silva Equipment Repair**

(a), (c) and (e) (Continued)

Supplies Expense — No. 615

| Date | Explanation | Ref. | Debit | Credit | Balance |
|---|---|---|---|---|---|
| | | | | | |
| | | | | | |

Salaries Expense — No. 726

| Date | Explanation | Ref. | Debit | Credit | Balance |
|---|---|---|---|---|---|
| | | | | | |
| | | | | | |
| | | | | | |
| | | | | | |

Rent Expense — No. 729

| Date | Explanation | Ref. | Debit | Credit | Balance |
|---|---|---|---|---|---|
| | | | | | |
| | | | | | |

(b)

General Journal — J1

| | Date | Account Titles and Explanation | Ref. | Debit | Credit | |
|---|---|---|---|---|---|---|
| 1 | | | | | | 1 |
| 2 | | | | | | 2 |
| 3 | | | | | | 3 |
| 4 | | | | | | 4 |
| 5 | | | | | | 5 |
| 6 | | | | | | 6 |
| 7 | | | | | | 7 |
| 8 | | | | | | 8 |
| 9 | | | | | | 9 |
| 10 | | | | | | 10 |
| 11 | | | | | | 11 |
| 12 | | | | | | 12 |
| 13 | | | | | | 13 |
| 14 | | | | | | 14 |
| 15 | | | | | | 15 |
| 16 | | | | | | 16 |
| 17 | | | | | | 17 |
| 18 | | | | | | 18 |
| 19 | | | | | | 19 |
| 20 | | | | | | 20 |

Name

Section

Date

**Problem 3-5B Continued**

**Silva Equipment Repair**

(b)(Continued) General Journal J1

| Date | Account Titles and Explanation | Ref. | Debit | Credit |
|---|---|---|---|---|
| | | | | |
| | | | | |
| | | | | |
| | | | | |
| | | | | |
| | | | | |
| | | | | |
| | | | | |
| | | | | |
| | | | | |
| | | | | |
| | | | | |
| | | | | |
| | | | | |
| | | | | |
| | | | | |
| | | | | |

(e) General Journal J2

| Date | Account Titles and Explanation | Ref. | Debit | Credit |
|---|---|---|---|---|
| | | | | |
| | | | | |
| | | | | |
| | | | | |
| | | | | |
| | | | | |
| | | | | |
| | | | | |
| | | | | |
| | | | | |
| | | | | |
| | | | | |
| | | | | |
| | | | | |
| | | | | |
| | | | | |

Name

Section

Date

**Problem 3-5B Continued**

**Silva Equipment Repair**

(d) and (f)

SILVA EQUIPMENT REPAIR

Trial Balances

September 30, 1999

| | Before Adjustment | | After Adjustment | |
|---|---|---|---|---|
| | Dr. | Cr. | Dr. | Cr. |

(g)

SILVA EQUIPMENT REPAIR

Income Statement

For the Month Ended September 30, 1999

(g) (Continued)

SILVA EQUIPMENT REPAIR

Owner's Equity Statement

For the Month Ended September 30, 1999

SILVA EQUIPMENT REPAIR

Balance Sheet

September 30, 1999

Assets

Liabilities and Owner's Equity

Name
Section
Date

(a)

(b)

(c)

Name

Section

Date

**Kellogg vs. General Mills**

| Increase (decrease) from 1996 to 1997 (in thousands) in | Kellogg | General Mills |
|---|---|---|
| (a) Property, plant, and equipment, net | | |
| (b) Selling, general, and administrative expense | | |
| (c) Accounts payable | | |
| (d) Net income | | |
| (e) Cash and cash equivalents | | |

Name

Section

Date



(a)

(b)

Name

Section

Date



(a)

HAPPY TRAVEL COURT

Income Statement

For the Quarter Ended March 31, 1999

(b)

Name

Section

Date



**REAL-WORLD FOCUS** Laser Recording Systems Incorporated

(a)

(b)

(c)

**ETHICS CASE** Die Hard Company

(a)

(b)

(c)

Name

Section

Date

Name

Section

Date



**Warren Company**

WARREN COMPANY

Work Sheet

| | Account Titles | Trial Balance | | Adjusting Entries | | Adjusted Trial Balance | | Income Statement | | Balance Sheet | | |
|---|---|---|---|---|---|---|---|---|---|---|---|---|
| | | Debit | Credit | Debit | Credit | Debit | Credit | Debit | Credit | Debit | Credit | |
| 1 | | | | | | | | | | | | 1 |
| 2 | | | | | | | | | | | | 2 |
| 3 | | | | | | | | | | | | 3 |
| 4 | | | | | | | | | | | | 4 |
| 5 | | | | | | | | | | | | 5 |
| 6 | | | | | | | | | | | | 6 |
| 7 | | | | | | | | | | | | 7 |
| 8 | | | | | | | | | | | | 8 |
| 9 | | | | | | | | | | | | 9 |
| 10 | | | | | | | | | | | | 10 |
| 11 | | | | | | | | | | | | 11 |
| 12 | | | | | | | | | | | | 12 |
| 13 | | | | | | | | | | | | 13 |
| 14 | | | | | | | | | | | | 14 |
| 15 | | | | | | | | | | | | 15 |
| 16 | | | | | | | | | | | | 16 |
| 17 | | | | | | | | | | | | 17 |
| 18 | | | | | | | | | | | | 18 |
| 19 | | | | | | | | | | | | 19 |
| 20 | | | | | | | | | | | | 20 |
| 21 | | | | | | | | | | | | 21 |
| 22 | | | | | | | | | | | | 22 |
| 23 | | | | | | | | | | | | 23 |
| 24 | | | | | | | | | | | | 24 |

Name

Section

Date

| Date | Explanation | Ref. | Debit | Credit | Balance |
| --- | --- | --- | --- | --- | --- |
| | | | | | |
| | | | | | |
| | | | | | |

| Date | Explanation | Ref. | Debit | Credit | Balance |
| --- | --- | --- | --- | --- | --- |
| | | | | | |
| | | | | | |
| | | | | | |

Name

Section

Date

Name

Section

Date

Name

Section

Date

**Exercise 4-1**

**Jose Navarro Company**

**JOSE NAVARRO COMPANY**

Work Sheet (Partial)

For the Month Ended April 30, 1999

| | Account Titles | Adjusted Trial Balance | | Income Statement | | Balance Sheet | | |
|---|---|---|---|---|---|---|---|---|
| | | Dr. | Cr. | Dr. | Cr. | Dr. | Cr. | |
| 1 | | | | | | | | 1 |
| 2 | | | | | | | | 2 |
| 3 | | | | | | | | 3 |
| 4 | | | | | | | | 4 |
| 5 | | | | | | | | 5 |
| 6 | | | | | | | | 6 |
| 7 | | | | | | | | 7 |
| 8 | | | | | | | | 8 |
| 9 | | | | | | | | 9 |
| 10 | | | | | | | | 10 |
| 11 | | | | | | | | 11 |
| 12 | | | | | | | | 12 |
| 13 | | | | | | | | 13 |
| 14 | | | | | | | | 14 |
| 15 | | | | | | | | 15 |
| 16 | | | | | | | | 16 |
| 17 | | | | | | | | 17 |
| 18 | | | | | | | | 18 |
| 19 | | | | | | | | 19 |
| 20 | | | | | | | | 20 |
| 21 | | | | | | | | 21 |
| 22 | | | | | | | | 22 |
| 23 | | | | | | | | 23 |
| 24 | | | | | | | | 24 |
| 25 | | | | | | | | 25 |

Name | **Exercise 4-2**

Section

Date | **Jose Navarro Company**

JOSE NAVARRO COMPANY
Income Statement
For the Month Ended April 30, 1999

JOSE NAVARRO COMPANY
Owner's Equity Statement
For the Month Ended April 30, 1999

JOSE NAVARRO COMPANY
Balance Sheet
April 30, 1999

Assets

Liabilities and Owner's Equity

Name

Section

Date

**Exercise 4-3**

**Jose Navarro Company**

(a)

(b)

INCOME SUMMARY

J. NAVARRO, CAPITAL

(c)

JOSE NAVARRO COMPANY
Post-Closing Trial Balance
April 30, 1999

| | Debit | Credit |
|---|---|---|
| | | |

Name

Section

Date

#4

#5

Name

Section

Date

**Exercise 4-**

**Raphael Company**

(a)

General Journal

| | Date | Account Titles and Explanation | Ref. | Debit | Credit | |
|---|---|---|---|---|---|---|
| 1 | | | | | | 1 |
| 2 | | | | | | 2 |
| 3 | | | | | | 3 |
| 4 | | | | | | 4 |
| 5 | | | | | | 5 |
| 6 | | | | | | 6 |
| 7 | | | | | | 7 |
| 8 | | | | | | 8 |
| 9 | | | | | | 9 |
| 10 | | | | | | 10 |
| 11 | | | | | | 11 |
| 12 | | | | | | 12 |
| 13 | | | | | | 13 |
| 14 | | | | | | 14 |

(b)

S. Raphael, Capital — No. 301

| Date | Explanation | Ref. | Debit | Credit | Balance |
|---|---|---|---|---|---|
| | | | | | |
| | | | | | |
| | | | | | |
| | | | | | |

Income Summary — No. 350

| Date | Explanation | Ref. | Debit | Credit | Balance |
|---|---|---|---|---|---|
| | | | | | |
| | | | | | |
| | | | | | |
| | | | | | |

(c)

RAPHAEL COMPANY

Post-Closing Trial Balance

July 31, 1999

| | | Debit | Credit | |
|---|---|---|---|---|
| 1 | | | | 1 |
| 2 | | | | 2 |
| 3 | | | | 3 |
| 4 | | | | 4 |
| 5 | | | | 5 |
| 6 | | | | 6 |
| 7 | | | | 7 |
| 8 | | | | 8 |
| 9 | | | | 9 |

Name **Exercise 4-7**

Section

Date **Raphael Company**

(a)

RAPHAEL COMPANY

Income Statement

For the Year Ended July 31, 1999

RAPHAEL COMPANY

Owner's Equity Statement

For the Year Ended July 31, 1999

(b)

RAPHAEL COMPANY

Balance Sheet

July 31, 1999

Assets

Liabilities and Owner's Equity

Name

Section

Date



**#8**

(a)

(b)

INCOME SUMMARY

**#9**

Name | Exercise 4-10

Section

Date | Bel-Air Bowling Alley

(a)

BEL-AIR BOWLING ALLEY
Balance Sheet
December 31, 1999

| | | |
|---|---|---|
| Assets | | |
| | | |
| | | |
| | | |
| | | |
| | | |
| | | |
| | | |
| | | |
| | | |
| | | |
| | | |
| | | |
| | | |
| | | |
| Liabilities and Owner's Equity | | |
| | | |
| | | |
| | | |
| | | |
| | | |
| | | |
| | | |
| | | |
| | | |
| | | |
| | | |
| | | |
| | | |
| | | |

(b)

Name

Section

Date

***Exercise 4-1**

**Garrett Employment Agency**

(a)

(b)

(c/e)

ACCOUNTS RECEIVABLE

COMMISSION REVENUE

INTEREST PAYABLE

INTEREST EXPENSE

(d)

Additional working papers for this problem are at the back of this book.

(b)

SPELLMAN ROOFING
Income Statement
For the Month Ended March 31, 1999

SPELLMAN ROOFING
Owner's Equity Statement
For the Month Ended March 31, 1999

(b) (Continued)

SPELLMAN ROOFING
Balance Sheet
March 31, 1999

| | | |
|---|---|---|
| Assets | | |
| Liabilities and Owner's Equity | | |

 

Name

Section

Date

**Problem 4-1A Concluded**

**Spellman Roofing**

(c)

General Journal

| | Date | Account Titles and Explanation | Ref. | Debit | Credit | |
|---|---|---|---|---|---|---|
| 1 | | Adjusting Entries | | | | 1 |
| 2 | | | | | | 2 |
| 3 | | | | | | 3 |
| 4 | | | | | | 4 |
| 5 | | | | | | 5 |
| 6 | | | | | | 6 |
| 7 | | | | | | 7 |
| 8 | | | | | | 8 |
| 9 | | | | | | 9 |
| 10 | | | | | | 10 |
| 11 | | | | | | 11 |
| 12 | | | | | | 12 |
| 13 | | | | | | 13 |
| 14 | | | | | | 14 |
| 15 | | | | | | 15 |
| 16 | | | | | | 16 |

(d)

General Journal

| | Date | Account Titles and Explanation | Ref. | Debit | Credit | |
|---|---|---|---|---|---|---|
| 1 | | Closing Entries | | | | 1 |
| 2 | | | | | | 2 |
| 3 | | | | | | 3 |
| 4 | | | | | | 4 |
| 5 | | | | | | 5 |
| 6 | | | | | | 6 |
| 7 | | | | | | 7 |
| 8 | | | | | | 8 |
| 9 | | | | | | 9 |
| 10 | | | | | | 10 |
| 11 | | | | | | 11 |
| 12 | | | | | | 12 |
| 13 | | | | | | 13 |
| 14 | | | | | | 14 |
| 15 | | | | | | 15 |
| 16 | | | | | | 16 |

Name
Section
Date

**Problem 4-2A**

**Perez Company**

(a)

PEREZ COMPANY
Work Sheet (Partial)
For the Year Ended December 31, 1999

| | Account | | Adjusted Trial Balance | | Income Statement | | Balance Sheet | | |
|---|---|---|---|---|---|---|---|---|---|
| | No. | Title | Dr. | Cr. | Dr. | Cr. | Dr. | Cr. | |
| 1 | | | | | | | | | 1 |
| 2 | | | | | | | | | 2 |
| 3 | | | | | | | | | 3 |
| 4 | | | | | | | | | 4 |
| 5 | | | | | | | | | 5 |
| 6 | | | | | | | | | 6 |
| 7 | | | | | | | | | 7 |
| 8 | | | | | | | | | 8 |
| 9 | | | | | | | | | 9 |
| 10 | | | | | | | | | 10 |
| 11 | | | | | | | | | 11 |
| 12 | | | | | | | | | 12 |
| 13 | | | | | | | | | 13 |
| 14 | | | | | | | | | 14 |
| 15 | | | | | | | | | 15 |
| 16 | | | | | | | | | 16 |
| 17 | | | | | | | | | 17 |
| 18 | | | | | | | | | 18 |
| 19 | | | | | | | | | 19 |
| 20 | | | | | | | | | 20 |
| 21 | | | | | | | | | 21 |
| 22 | | | | | | | | | 22 |
| 23 | | | | | | | | | 23 |
| 24 | | | | | | | | | 24 |
| 25 | | | | | | | | | 25 |
| 26 | | | | | | | | | 26 |
| 27 | | | | | | | | | 27 |
| 28 | | | | | | | | | 28 |

Name

Section

Date



(b)

PEREZ COMPANY
Income Statement
For the Year Ended December 31, 1999

| | | | |
|---|---|---|---|
| 1 | | | |
| 2 | | | |
| 3 | | | |
| 4 | | | |
| 5 | | | |
| 6 | | | |
| 7 | | | |
| 8 | | | |
| 9 | | | |
| 10 | | | |
| 11 | | | |
| 12 | | | |
| 13 | | | |
| 14 | | | |
| 15 | | | |

PEREZ COMPANY
Owner's Equity Statement
For the Year Ended December 31, 1999

| | | | |
|---|---|---|---|
| 1 | | | |
| 2 | | | |
| 3 | | | |
| 4 | | | |
| 5 | | | |
| 6 | | | |
| 7 | | | |
| 8 | | | |
| 9 | | | |
| 10 | | | |

(b) (Continued)

PEREZ COMPANY
Balance Sheet
December 31, 1999

| | | |
|---|---|---|
| Assets | | |
| | | |
| | | |
| | | |
| | | |
| | | |
| | | |
| | | |
| | | |
| | | |
| | | |
| | | |
| | | |
| | | |
| | | |
| Liabilities and Owner's Equity | | |
| | | |
| | | |
| | | |
| | | |
| | | |
| | | |
| | | |
| | | |
| | | |
| | | |
| | | |
| | | |
| | | |
| | | |

Name | **Problem 4-2A Continued**
Section
Date | **Perez Company**

(c) General Journal J14

| | Date | Account Titles and Explanation | Ref. | Debit | Credit | |
|---|---|---|---|---|---|---|
| 1 | | Closing Entries | | | | 1 |
| 2 | | | | | | 2 |
| 3 | | | | | | 3 |
| 4 | | | | | | 4 |
| 5 | | | | | | 5 |
| 6 | | | | | | 6 |
| 7 | | | | | | 7 |
| 8 | | | | | | 8 |
| 9 | | | | | | 9 |
| 10 | | | | | | 10 |
| 11 | | | | | | 11 |
| 12 | | | | | | 12 |
| 13 | | | | | | 13 |
| 14 | | | | | | 14 |
| 15 | | | | | | 15 |
| 16 | | | | | | 16 |
| 17 | | | | | | 17 |
| 18 | | | | | | 18 |

(d) J. Perez, Capital No. 301

| Date | Explanation | Ref. | Debit | Credit | Balance |
|---|---|---|---|---|---|
| | | | | | |
| | | | | | |
| | | | | | |
| | | | | | |

J. Perez, Drawing No. 306

| Date | Explanation | Ref. | Debit | Credit | Balance |
|---|---|---|---|---|---|
| | | | | | |
| | | | | | |
| | | | | | |

Income Summary No. 350

| Date | Explanation | Ref. | Debit | Credit | Balance |
|---|---|---|---|---|---|
| | | | | | |
| | | | | | |
| | | | | | |
| | | | | | |

Name

Section

Date

**Problem 4-2A Continued**

**Perez Company**

(d) (Continued)

Service Revenue — No. 400

| Date | Explanation | Ref. | Debit | Credit | Balance |
|---|---|---|---|---|---|
| | | | | | |
| | | | | | |
| | | | | | |

Advertising Expense — No. 610

| Date | Explanation | Ref. | Debit | Credit | Balance |
|---|---|---|---|---|---|
| | | | | | |
| | | | | | |
| | | | | | |

Supplies Expense — No. 631

| Date | Explanation | Ref. | Debit | Credit | Balance |
|---|---|---|---|---|---|
| | | | | | |
| | | | | | |
| | | | | | |

Depreciation Expense — No. 711

| Date | Explanation | Ref. | Debit | Credit | Balance |
|---|---|---|---|---|---|
| | | | | | |
| | | | | | |
| | | | | | |

Interest Expense — No. 718

| Date | Explanation | Ref. | Debit | Credit | Balance |
|---|---|---|---|---|---|
| | | | | | |
| | | | | | |
| | | | | | |

Insurance Expense — No. 722

| Date | Explanation | Ref. | Debit | Credit | Balance |
|---|---|---|---|---|---|
| | | | | | |
| | | | | | |
| | | | | | |

Name

Section

Date

**Problem 4-2A Concluded**

**Perez Company**

(d) (Continued)

Salaries Expense — No. 726

| Date | Explanation | Ref. | Debit | Credit | Balance |
|---|---|---|---|---|---|
| | | | | | |
| | | | | | |
| | | | | | |

(e)

PEREZ COMPANY
Post-Closing Trial Balance
December 31, 1999

| | | Debit | Credit | |
|---|---|---|---|---|
| 1 | | | | 1 |
| 2 | | | | 2 |
| 3 | | | | 3 |
| 4 | | | | 4 |
| 5 | | | | 5 |
| 6 | | | | 6 |
| 7 | | | | 7 |
| 8 | | | | 8 |
| 9 | | | | 9 |
| 10 | | | | 10 |
| 11 | | | | 11 |
| 12 | | | | 12 |
| 13 | | | | 13 |
| 14 | | | | 14 |
| 15 | | | | 15 |
| 16 | | | | 16 |
| 17 | | | | 17 |
| 18 | | | | 18 |
| 19 | | | | 19 |
| 20 | | | | 20 |

Name

Section

Date

**Problem 4-3A**

**Strug Company**

(a)

STRUG COMPANY

Income Statement

For the Year Ended December 31, 1999

STRUG COMPANY

Balance Sheet

December 31, 1999

Assets

Liabilities and Owner's Equity

Name

Section

Date

**Problem 4-3A Continued**

**Strug Company**

(a) (Continued)

STRUG COMPANY

Owner's Equity Statement

For the Year Ended December 31, 1999

(b) General Journal

| Date | Account Titles | Ref. | Debit | Credit |
|---|---|---|---|---|
| | Closing Entries | | | |

Name
Section
Date

**Problem 4-3A Concluded**

**Strug Company**

(c)

General Ledger Accounts

| K. Strug, Capital No. 301 | Repair Expense No. 622 |
|---|---|
| K. Strug, Drawing No. 306 | Depreciation Expense No. 711 |
| Income Summary No. 350 | Insurance Expense No. 722 |
| Service Revenue No. 400 | Salaries Expense No. 726 |
| | Utilities Expense No. 732 |

(d)

STRUG COMPANY
Post-Closing Trial Balance
December 31, 1999

| | | Debit | Credit |
|---|---|---|---|
| 1 | | | |
| 2 | | | |
| 3 | | | |
| 4 | | | |
| 5 | | | |
| 6 | | | |
| 7 | | | |
| 8 | | | |
| 9 | | | |
| 10 | | | |
| 11 | | | |
| 12 | | | |

Additional working papers for this problem are at the back of this book.

(b)

LOGAN MANAGEMENT SERVICES
Balance Sheet
December 31, 1999

Assets

Liabilities and Owner's Equity

Name

Section

Date

**Problem 4-4A Continued**

**Logan Management Services**

(c) and (d)

General Journal

| Date | Account Titles and Explanation | Ref. | Debit | Credit |
|---|---|---|---|---|
| (c) | Adjusting Entries | | | |
| | | | | |
| | | | | |
| | | | | |
| | | | | |
| | | | | |
| | | | | |
| | | | | |
| | | | | |
| | | | | |
| | | | | |
| | | | | |
| | | | | |
| | | | | |
| | | | | |
| | | | | |
| | | | | |
| | | | | |
| (d) | Closing Entries | | | |
| | | | | |
| | | | | |
| | | | | |
| | | | | |
| | | | | |
| | | | | |
| | | | | |
| | | | | |
| | | | | |
| | | | | |
| | | | | |
| | | | | |
| | | | | |
| | | | | |
| | | | | |
| | | | | |
| | | | | |
| | | | | |
| | | | | |
| | | | | |
| | | | | |

LOGAN MANAGEMENT SERVICES
Post-Closing Trial Balance
December 31, 1999

(e)

| | Debit | Credit |
|---|---|---|
| | | |

Name

Section

Date

**Problem 4-5A**

**Jill's Window Washing**

(a)

General Journal

J1

| Date | Account Titles and Explanation | Ref. | Debit | Credit |
|---|---|---|---|---|

Name

Section

Date

**Problem 4-5A Continued**

**Jill's Window Washing**

(a), (e) and (f)

Cash — No. 101

| Date | Explanation | Ref. | Debit | Credit | Balance |
|---|---|---|---|---|---|
| | | | | | |
| | | | | | |
| | | | | | |
| | | | | | |
| | | | | | |
| | | | | | |
| | | | | | |
| | | | | | |
| | | | | | |

Accounts Receivable — No. 112

| Date | Explanation | Ref. | Debit | Credit | Balance |
|---|---|---|---|---|---|
| | | | | | |
| | | | | | |
| | | | | | |
| | | | | | |
| | | | | | |
| | | | | | |

Cleaning Supplies — No. 128

| Date | Explanation | Ref. | Debit | Credit | Balance |
|---|---|---|---|---|---|
| | | | | | |
| | | | | | |
| | | | | | |

Prepaid Insurance — No. 130

| Date | Explanation | Ref. | Debit | Credit | Balance |
|---|---|---|---|---|---|
| | | | | | |
| | | | | | |
| | | | | | |

Equipment — No. 157

| Date | Explanation | Ref. | Debit | Credit | Balance |
|---|---|---|---|---|---|
| | | | | | |
| | | | | | |
| | | | | | |

Name
Section
Date

**Problem 4-5A Continued**

**Jill's Window Washing**

(a), (e) and (f) (Continued)

Accumulated Depreciation — Equipment

No. 158

| Date | Explanation | Ref. | Debit | Credit | Balance |
|---|---|---|---|---|---|
| | | | | | |
| | | | | | |

Accounts Payable

No. 201

| Date | Explanation | Ref. | Debit | Credit | Balance |
|---|---|---|---|---|---|
| | | | | | |
| | | | | | |
| | | | | | |
| | | | | | |

Salaries Payable

No. 212

| Date | Explanation | Ref. | Debit | Credit | Balance |
|---|---|---|---|---|---|
| | | | | | |
| | | | | | |

Jill Marsh, Capital

No. 301

| Date | Explanation | Ref. | Debit | Credit | Balance |
|---|---|---|---|---|---|
| | | | | | |
| | | | | | |
| | | | | | |
| | | | | | |

Jill Marsh, Drawing

No. 306

| Date | Explanation | Ref. | Debit | Credit | Balance |
|---|---|---|---|---|---|
| | | | | | |
| | | | | | |
| | | | | | |

Income Summary

No. 350

| Date | Explanation | Ref. | Debit | Credit | Balance |
|---|---|---|---|---|---|
| | | | | | |
| | | | | | |
| | | | | | |
| | | | | | |
| | | | | | |

(a), (e) and (f) (Continued)

Service Revenue — No. 400

| Date | Explanation | Ref. | Debit | Credit | Balance |
|---|---|---|---|---|---|
| | | | | | |
| | | | | | |
| | | | | | |
| | | | | | |
| | | | | | |

Gas & Oil Expense — No. 633

| Date | Explanation | Ref. | Debit | Credit | Balance |
|---|---|---|---|---|---|
| | | | | | |
| | | | | | |
| | | | | | |

Cleaning Supplies Expense — No. 634

| Date | Explanation | Ref. | Debit | Credit | Balance |
|---|---|---|---|---|---|
| | | | | | |
| | | | | | |
| | | | | | |

Depreciation Expense — No. 711

| Date | Explanation | Ref. | Debit | Credit | Balance |
|---|---|---|---|---|---|
| | | | | | |
| | | | | | |
| | | | | | |

Insurance Expense — No. 722

| Date | Explanation | Ref. | Debit | Credit | Balance |
|---|---|---|---|---|---|
| | | | | | |
| | | | | | |
| | | | | | |

Salaries Expense — No. 726

| Date | Explanation | Ref. | Debit | Credit | Balance |
|---|---|---|---|---|---|
| | | | | | |
| | | | | | |
| | | | | | |
| | | | | | |

Additional working papers for this problem are at the back of this book.

(d)

JILL'S WINDOW WASHING

Income Statement

For the Month Ended July 31, 1999

JILL'S WINDOW WASHING

Owner's Equity Statement

For the Month Ended July 31, 1999

Name

Section

Date

**Problem 4-5A Continued**

**Jill's Window Washing**

(d) (Continued)

JILL'S WINDOW WASHING

Balance Sheet

July 31, 1999

| | | |
|---|---|---|
| Assets | | |
| | | |
| | | |
| | | |
| | | |
| | | |
| | | |
| | | |
| | | |
| | | |
| | | |
| | | |
| | | |
| Liabilities and Owner's Equity | | |
| | | |
| | | |
| | | |
| | | |
| | | |
| | | |
| | | |
| | | |

(g)

JILL'S WINDOW WASHING

Post-Closing Trial Balance

July 31, 1999

| | Debit | Credit |
|---|---|---|
| | | |
| | | |
| | | |
| | | |
| | | |
| | | |
| | | |
| | | |
| | | |
| | | |
| | | |
| | | |

Name

Section

Date

**Problem 4-5A Concluded**

**Jill's Window Washing**

(e) and (f)

General Journal

J2–J3

| Date | Account Titles and Explanation | Ref. | Debit | Credit |
|---|---|---|---|---|
| (e) | Adjusting Entries | | | |
| (f) | Closing Entries | | | |

Name

Section

Date

**Problem 4-6A Concluded**

**Everlast TV Repair**

Additional working papers for this problem are at the back of this book.

(b)

EVERLAST TV REPAIR

Trial Balance

April 30, 1999

| | Debit | Credit |
|---|---|---|
| | | |

Name
Section
Date

**Problem 4-1B Continued**

**Columbo P.I.**

Additional working papers for this problem are at the back of this book.

(b)

COLUMBO P.I.
Income Statement
For the Quarter Ended March 31, 1999

COLUMBO P.I.
Owner's Equity Statement
For the Quarter Ended March 31, 1999

(b) (Continued)

COLUMBO P.I.
Balance Sheet
March 31, 1999

Assets

Liabilities and Owner's Equity

(c)

General Journal

| Date | Account Titles and Explanation | Ref. | Debit | Credit |
|---|---|---|---|---|
| | Adjusting Entries | | | |
| | | | | |
| | | | | |
| | | | | |
| | | | | |
| | | | | |
| | | | | |
| | | | | |
| | | | | |
| | | | | |
| | | | | |
| | | | | |
| | | | | |
| | | | | |
| | | | | |
| | | | | |

(d)

General Journal

| Date | Account Titles and Explanation | Ref. | Debit | Credit |
|---|---|---|---|---|
| | Closing Entries | | | |
| | | | | |
| | | | | |
| | | | | |
| | | | | |
| | | | | |
| | | | | |
| | | | | |
| | | | | |
| | | | | |
| | | | | |
| | | | | |
| | | | | |
| | | | | |
| | | | | |
| | | | | |
| | | | | |
| | | | | |
| | | | | |

Name | **Problem 4-2B**

Section

Date | **Oslo Company**

(a)

OSLO COMPANY
Work Sheet (Partial)
For the Year Ended December 31, 1999

| Account | | Adjusted Trial Balance | | Income Statement | | Balance Sheet | |
|---|---|---|---|---|---|---|---|
| No. | Titles | Dr. | Cr. | Dr. | Cr. | Dr. | Cr. |

(b)

OSLO COMPANY
Income Statement
For the Year Ended December 31, 1999

OSLO COMPANY
Owner's Equity Statement
For the Year Ended December 31, 1999

Name

Section

Date

**Problem 4-2B Continued**

**Oslo Company**

(b) (Continued)

OSLO COMPANY
Balance Sheet
December 31, 1999

Assets

Liabilities and Owner's Equity

Name

Section

Date

**Problem 4-2B Continued**

**Oslo Company**

(c) General Journal J14

| Date | Account Titles and Explanation | Ref. | Debit | Credit |
|---|---|---|---|---|
| | Closing Entries | | | |

d)

S. Oslo, Capital — No. 301

| Date | Explanation | Ref. | Debit | Credit | Balance |
|---|---|---|---|---|---|
| | | | | | |
| | | | | | |
| | | | | | |
| | | | | | |

S. Oslo, Drawing — No. 306

| Date | Explanation | Ref. | Debit | Credit | Balance |
|---|---|---|---|---|---|
| | | | | | |
| | | | | | |
| | | | | | |

Income Summary — No. 350

| Date | Explanation | Ref. | Debit | Credit | Balance |
|---|---|---|---|---|---|
| | | | | | |
| | | | | | |
| | | | | | |
| | | | | | |

Service Revenue — No. 400

| Date | Explanation | Ref. | Debit | Credit | Balance |
|---|---|---|---|---|---|
| | | | | | |
| | | | | | |
| | | | | | |

Advertising Expense — No. 610

| Date | Explanation | Ref. | Debit | Credit | Balance |
|---|---|---|---|---|---|
| | | | | | |
| | | | | | |
| | | | | | |

Supplies Expense — No. 631

| Date | Explanation | Ref. | Debit | Credit | Balance |
|---|---|---|---|---|---|
| | | | | | |
| | | | | | |
| | | | | | |

Name

Section

Date



(d) (Continued)

Depreciation Expense — No. 71

| Date | Explanation | Ref. | Debit | Credit | Balance |
|---|---|---|---|---|---|
| | | | | | |
| | | | | | |
| | | | | | |

Insurance Expense — No. 72

| Date | Explanation | Ref. | Debit | Credit | Balance |
|---|---|---|---|---|---|
| | | | | | |
| | | | | | |
| | | | | | |

Salaries Expense — No. 726

| Date | Explanation | Ref. | Debit | Credit | Balance |
|---|---|---|---|---|---|
| | | | | | |
| | | | | | |
| | | | | | |

Interest Expense — No. 905

| Date | Explanation | Ref. | Debit | Credit | Balance |
|---|---|---|---|---|---|
| | | | | | |
| | | | | | |
| | | | | | |

(e)

OSLO COMPANY
Post-Closing Trial Balance
December 31, 1999

| | | Debit | Credit | |
|---|---|---|---|---|
| 1 | | | | 1 |
| 2 | | | | 2 |
| 3 | | | | 3 |
| 4 | | | | 4 |
| 5 | | | | 5 |
| 6 | | | | 6 |
| 7 | | | | 7 |
| 8 | | | | 8 |
| 9 | | | | 9 |
| 10 | | | | 10 |
| 11 | | | | 11 |
| 12 | | | | 12 |
| 13 | | | | 13 |
| 14 | | | | 14 |

Name

Section

Date

**Problem 4-3B**

**Sierra Company**

(a)

SIERRA COMPANY

Income Statement

For the Year Ended December 31, 1999

SIERRA COMPANY

Owner's Equity Statement

For the Year Ended December 31, 1999

(a) (Continued)

SIERRA COMPANY
Balance Sheet
December 31, 1999

Assets

Liabilities and Owner's Equity

(b) General Journal

| Date | Account Titles and Explanation | Ref. | Debit | Credit |
|---|---|---|---|---|
| | | | | |

 

Name

Section

Date

**Problem 4-3B Concluded**

**Sierra Company**

(c)

General Ledger Accounts

M. Sierra, Capital No. 301

M. Sierra, Drawing No. 306

Income Summary No. 350

Service Revenue No. 400

Repair Expense No. 622

Depreciation Expense No. 711

Insurance Expense No. 722

Salaries Expense No. 726

Utilities Expense No. 732

(d)

SIERRA COMPANY
Post-Closing Trial Balance
December 31, 1999

| | Debit | Credit |
|---|---|---|
| | | |
| | | |
| | | |
| | | |
| | | |
| | | |
| | | |
| | | |
| | | |
| | | |
| | | |
| | | |

Additional working papers for this problem are at the back of this book.

(b)

WATERWORLD AMUSEMENT PARK

Balance Sheet

September 30, 1999

Assets

Liabilities and Owner's Equity

Name

Section

Date

**Problem 4-4B Continued**

**Waterworld Amusement Park**

(c) and (d)

General Journal

| Date | Account Titles and Explanation | Ref. | Debit | Credit |
|---|---|---|---|---|
| (c) | Adjusting Entries | | | |
| (d) | Closing Entries | | | |

(e)

WATERWORLD AMUSEMENT PARK
Post-Closing Trial Balance
September 30, 1999

| | Debit | Credit |
|---|---|---|

 

Name | **Problem 4-5B**

Section

Date | **Anna's Carpet Cleaners**

Additional working papers for this problem are at the back of this book.

(a) General Journal J1

| Date | Account Titles and Explanation | Ref. | Debit | Credit |
|---|---|---|---|---|

Name
Section
Date

**Problem 4-5B Continued**

**Anna's Carpet Cleaners**

(a), (e) and (f)

Cash — No. 101

| Date | Explanation | Ref. | Debit | Credit | Balance |
|---|---|---|---|---|---|
| | | | | | |
| | | | | | |
| | | | | | |
| | | | | | |
| | | | | | |
| | | | | | |
| | | | | | |
| | | | | | |
| | | | | | |

Accounts Receivable — No. 112

| Date | Explanation | Ref. | Debit | Credit | Balance |
|---|---|---|---|---|---|
| | | | | | |
| | | | | | |
| | | | | | |
| | | | | | |
| | | | | | |

Cleaning Supplies — No. 128

| Date | Explanation | Ref. | Debit | Credit | Balance |
|---|---|---|---|---|---|
| | | | | | |
| | | | | | |
| | | | | | |

Prepaid Insurance — No. 130

| Date | Explanation | Ref. | Debit | Credit | Balance |
|---|---|---|---|---|---|
| | | | | | |
| | | | | | |
| | | | | | |

Equipment — No. 157

| Date | Explanation | Ref. | Debit | Credit | Balance |
|---|---|---|---|---|---|
| | | | | | |
| | | | | | |

Accumulated Depreciation—Equipment — No. 158

| Date | Explanation | Ref. | Debit | Credit | Balance |
|---|---|---|---|---|---|
| | | | | | |
| | | | | | |

(a), (e) and (f) (Continued)

Accounts Payable No. 201

| Date | Explanation | Ref. | Debit | Credit | Balance |
| --- | --- | --- | --- | --- | --- |
| | | | | | |
| | | | | | |
| | | | | | |
| | | | | | |

Salaries Payable No. 212

| Date | Explanation | Ref. | Debit | Credit | Balance |
| --- | --- | --- | --- | --- | --- |
| | | | | | |
| | | | | | |

A. Khan, Capital No. 301

| Date | Explanation | Ref. | Debit | Credit | Balance |
| --- | --- | --- | --- | --- | --- |
| | | | | | |
| | | | | | |
| | | | | | |
| | | | | | |

A. Khan, Drawing No. 306

| Date | Explanation | Ref. | Debit | Credit | Balance |
| --- | --- | --- | --- | --- | --- |
| | | | | | |
| | | | | | |
| | | | | | |

Income Summary No. 350

| Date | Explanation | Ref. | Debit | Credit | Balance |
| --- | --- | --- | --- | --- | --- |
| | | | | | |
| | | | | | |
| | | | | | |
| | | | | | |

Service Revenue No. 400

| Date | Explanation | Ref. | Debit | Credit | Balance |
| --- | --- | --- | --- | --- | --- |
| | | | | | |
| | | | | | |
| | | | | | |
| | | | | | |
| | | | | | |

Name

Section

Date

**Problem 4-5B Continued**

**Anna's Carpet Cleaners**

(a), (e) and (f) (Continued)

Gas & Oil Expense — No. 633

| Date | Explanation | Ref. | Debit | Credit | Balance |
|---|---|---|---|---|---|
| | | | | | |
| | | | | | |
| | | | | | |

Cleaning Supplies Expense — No. 634

| Date | Explanation | Ref. | Debit | Credit | Balance |
|---|---|---|---|---|---|
| | | | | | |
| | | | | | |
| | | | | | |

Depreciation Expense — No. 711

| Date | Explanation | Ref. | Debit | Credit | Balance |
|---|---|---|---|---|---|
| | | | | | |
| | | | | | |
| | | | | | |

Insurance Expense — No. 722

| Date | Explanation | Ref. | Debit | Credit | Balance |
|---|---|---|---|---|---|
| | | | | | |
| | | | | | |
| | | | | | |

Salaries Expense — No. 726

| Date | Explanation | Ref. | Debit | Credit | Balance |
|---|---|---|---|---|---|
| | | | | | |
| | | | | | |
| | | | | | |
| | | | | | |

Name
Section
Date

**Problem 4-5B Continued**

**Anna's Carpet Cleaners**

(d)

ANNA'S CARPET CLEANERS
Income Statement
For the Month Ended March 31, 1999

ANNA'S CARPET CLEANERS
Owner's Equity Statement
For the Month Ended March 31, 1999

(d) (Continued)

ANNA'S CARPET CLEANERS
Balance Sheet
March 31, 1999

| | | |
|---|---|---|
| Assets | | |
| | | |
| | | |
| | | |
| | | |
| | | |
| | | |
| | | |
| | | |
| | | |
| | | |
| | | |
| Liabilities and Owner's Equity | | |
| | | |
| | | |
| | | |
| | | |
| | | |
| | | |
| | | |
| | | |
| | | |

(g)

ANNA'S CARPET CLEANERS
Post-Closing Trial Balance
March 31, 1999

| | Debit | Credit |
|---|---|---|
| | | |
| | | |
| | | |
| | | |
| | | |
| | | |
| | | |
| | | |
| | | |
| | | |
| | | |
| | | |

Name | **Problem 4-5B Continued**

Section

Date | **Anna's Carpet Cleaners**

(e) and (f) General Journal J2–J3

| Date | Account Titles and Explanation | Ref. | Debit | Credit |
|---|---|---|---|---|
| (e) | Adjusting Entries | | | |
| (f) | Closing Entries | | | |

Name

Section

Date



1.

2.

3.

4.

5.

Name

Section

Date

**Kellogg vs. General Mills**

| | Kellogg | General Mills |
|---|---|---|
| (a) In millions | | |
| 1. Total current assets | | |
| 2. Net property, plant, and equipment | | |
| 3. Total current liabilities | | |
| 4. Total stockholders' (shareholders') equity | | |

(b)

Name

Section

Date



**Case Corporation**

(a), (b), and (c)

(a)

(b)

| (c) General Ledger Account | Income Statement Item |
|---|---|

Name
Section
Date

Case Corporation

(d)

| | |
|---|---|
| Revenues | |
| Costs and expenses | |
| Income from operations before taxes | |

Name

Section

Date

(a)

CLEANFAST JANITORIAL SERVICE

Balance Sheet

December 31, 1999

Assets

Liabilities and Owner's Equity

Calculation of adjusted capital balance:

| | |
|---|---|
| Capital balance as reported | 54000 |

(b)

Name

Section



Date

**REAL-WORLD FOCUS** Bethlehem Corporation

(a)

(b)

(c)

**ETHICS CASE** Magnus Perfume Company

(a)

(b)

(c)

Name

Section

Date

Name

Section

Date

Name

Section

Date

Name

Section

Date

**Exercises 5-1 and 5-4**

General Journal

| Date | Account Titles and Explanation | Debit | Credit |
|---|---|---|---|
| **#1** | | | |
| **#4** | | | |

Name **Exercise 5-2**

Section

Date **College Office Supply**

General Journal

| Date | Account Titles and Explanation | Ref. | Debit | Credit |
|---|---|---|---|---|

Name

Section

Date

**Exercise 5-3**

**Arcadian Company**

General Journal

| Date | Account Titles and Explanation | Ref. | Debit | Credit |
|---|---|---|---|---|
| | | | | |
| | | | | |
| | | | | |
| | | | | |
| | | | | |
| | | | | |
| | | | | |
| | | | | |
| | | | | |
| | | | | |
| | | | | |
| | | | | |
| | | | | |
| | | | | |
| | | | | |
| | | | | |
| | | | | |
| | | | | |
| | | | | |
| | | | | |
| | | | | |
| | | | | |
| | | | | |
| | | | | |
| | | | | |
| | | | | |
| | | | | |
| | | | | |
| | | | | |
| | | | | |
| | | | | |
| | | | | |
| | | | | |
| | | | | |
| | | | | |
| | | | | |
| | | | | |
| | | | | |
| | | | | |
| | | | | |

Name

Section

Date



**#5** (a)

LOPEZ COMPANY
Income Statement (Partial)
For the Year Ended October 31, 1999

(b)

| | Debit | Credit |
| --- | --- | --- |

**#6**

| | Debit | Credit |
| --- | --- | --- |

Name

Section

Date

**Exercise 5-7**

**Alvarez Company**

ALVAREZ COMPANY
Work Sheet (Partial)
For the Period Ended May 31, 1999

| | Account Titles | Adjusted Trial Balance | | Income Statement | | Balance Sheet | | |
|---|---|---|---|---|---|---|---|---|
| | | Dr. | Cr. | Dr. | Cr. | Dr. | Cr. | |
| 1 | | | | | | | | 1 |
| 2 | | | | | | | | 2 |
| 3 | | | | | | | | 3 |
| 4 | | | | | | | | 4 |
| 5 | | | | | | | | 5 |
| 6 | | | | | | | | 6 |
| 7 | | | | | | | | 7 |
| 8 | | | | | | | | 8 |
| 9 | | | | | | | | 9 |
| 10 | | | | | | | | 10 |
| 11 | | | | | | | | 11 |
| 12 | | | | | | | | 12 |
| 13 | | | | | | | | 13 |
| 14 | | | | | | | | 14 |
| 15 | | | | | | | | 15 |
| 16 | | | | | | | | 16 |
| 17 | | | | | | | | 17 |
| 18 | | | | | | | | 18 |
| 19 | | | | | | | | 19 |
| 20 | | | | | | | | 20 |

Name | **Exercise 5-8**

Section

Date | **Acevedo Company**

(a)

ACEVEDO COMPANY

Income Statement

For the Year Ended December 31, 1999

(b)

ACEVEDO COMPANY

Income Statement

For the Year Ended December 31, 1999

Name

Section

Date



**#9**

**#10**

Name Problem 5-1A

Section

Date Carlos Hardware Store

(a) General Journal

| Date | Account Titles and Explanation | Ref. | Debit | Credit |
|---|---|---|---|---|
| | | | | |

(a) (Continued)

General Journal

| | Date | Account Titles and Explanation | Ref. | Debit | Credit | |
|---|---|---|---|---|---|---|
| 1 | | | | | | 1 |
| 2 | | | | | | 2 |
| 3 | | | | | | 3 |
| 4 | | | | | | 4 |
| 5 | | | | | | 5 |
| 6 | | | | | | 6 |
| 7 | | | | | | 7 |
| 8 | | | | | | 8 |
| 9 | | | | | | 9 |
| 10 | | | | | | 10 |
| 11 | | | | | | 11 |
| 12 | | | | | | 12 |
| 13 | | | | | | 13 |
| 14 | | | | | | 14 |
| 15 | | | | | | 15 |
| 16 | | | | | | 16 |

(b)

Cash No. 101

| Date | Explanation | Ref. | Debit | Credit | Balance |
|---|---|---|---|---|---|
| | | | | | |
| | | | | | |
| | | | | | |
| | | | | | |
| | | | | | |
| | | | | | |
| | | | | | |
| | | | | | |
| | | | | | |
| | | | | | |
| | | | | | |
| | | | | | |

Accounts Receivable No. 112

| Date | Explanation | Ref. | Debit | Credit | Balance |
|---|---|---|---|---|---|
| | | | | | |
| | | | | | |
| | | | | | |
| | | | | | |

Name
Section
Date

**Problem 5-1A Continued**

**Carlos Hardware Store**

(b) (Continued)

Merchandise Inventory — No. 120

| Date | Explanation | Ref. | Debit | Credit | Balance |
|---|---|---|---|---|---|
| | | | | | |
| | | | | | |
| | | | | | |
| | | | | | |
| | | | | | |
| | | | | | |
| | | | | | |
| | | | | | |
| | | | | | |
| | | | | | |
| | | | | | |
| | | | | | |
| | | | | | |
| | | | | | |

Supplies — No. 126

| Date | Explanation | Ref. | Debit | Credit | Balance |
|---|---|---|---|---|---|
| | | | | | |
| | | | | | |

Accounts Payable — No. 201

| Date | Explanation | Ref. | Debit | Credit | Balance |
|---|---|---|---|---|---|
| | | | | | |
| | | | | | |
| | | | | | |
| | | | | | |
| | | | | | |
| | | | | | |
| | | | | | |

J. Carlos, Capital — No. 301

| Date | Explanation | Ref. | Debit | Credit | Balance |
|---|---|---|---|---|---|
| | | | | | |
| | | | | | |
| | | | | | |

(b) (Continued)

Sales — No. 401

| Date | Explanation | Ref. | Debit | Credit | Balance |
|---|---|---|---|---|---|
| | | | | | |
| | | | | | |
| | | | | | |
| | | | | | |
| | | | | | |

Sales Returns and Allowances — No. 412

| Date | Explanation | Ref. | Debit | Credit | Balance |
|---|---|---|---|---|---|
| | | | | | |
| | | | | | |
| | | | | | |

Sales Discounts — No. 414

| Date | Explanation | Ref. | Debit | Credit | Balance |
|---|---|---|---|---|---|
| | | | | | |
| | | | | | |

Cost of Goods Sold — No. 505

| Date | Explanation | Ref. | Debit | Credit | Balance |
|---|---|---|---|---|---|
| | | | | | |
| | | | | | |
| | | | | | |
| | | | | | |
| | | | | | |

(c)

CARLOS HARDWARE STORE
Income Statement (Partial)
For the Month Ended May 31, 1999

| | | | | | | |
|---|---|---|---|---|---|---|
| 1 | | | | | | 1 |
| 2 | | | | | | 2 |
| 3 | | | | | | 3 |
| 4 | | | | | | 4 |
| 5 | | | | | | 5 |
| 6 | | | | | | 6 |
| 7 | | | | | | 7 |
| 8 | | | | | | 8 |
| 9 | | | | | | 9 |
| 10 | | | | | | 10 |

Name | Problem 5-2A

Section

Date | Anna Mossity Company

General Journal

| Date | Account Titles and Explanation | Ref. | Debit | Credit |
|---|---|---|---|---|
| | | | | |

Additional working papers for this problem are at the back of this book.

(b)

MONTY ZUMA WHOLESALE COMPANY
Income Statement
For the Year Ended December 31, 1999

Name

Section

Date

**Problem 5-3A Continued**

**Monty Zuma Wholesale Company**

(b) (Continued)

MONTY ZUMA WHOLESALE COMPANY
Owner's Equity Statement
For the Year Ended December 31, 1999

MONTY ZUMA WHOLESALE COMPANY
Balance Sheet
December 31, 1999

Assets

Liabilities and Owner's Equity

Name

Section

Date

**Problem 5-3A Continued**

**Monty Zuma Wholesale Company**

(c) and (d)

General Journal

| Date | Account Titles and Explanation | Ref. | Debit | Credit |
|---|---|---|---|---|
| (c) | Adjusting Entries | | | |
| (d) | Closing Entries | | | |

(d) (Continued)

General Journal

| Date | Account Titles and Explanation | Ref. | Debit | Credit |
|---|---|---|---|---|

(e)

MONTY ZUMA WHOLESALE COMPANY
Post-Closing Trial Balance
December 31, 1999

| | Debit | Credit |
|---|---|---|

Name

Section

Date

**Problem 5-4A**

**Rowbuck Department Store**

(a)

ROWBUCK DEPARTMENT STORE

Income Statement

For the Year Ended November 30, 1999

Name

Section

Date



(a) (Continued)

ROWBUCK DEPARTMENT STORE
Owner's Equity Statement
For the Year Ended November 30, 1999

| | | |
|---|---|---|
| 1 | | 1 |
| 2 | | 2 |
| 3 | | 3 |
| 4 | | 4 |
| 5 | | 5 |
| 6 | | 6 |

ROWBUCK DEPARTMENT STORE
Balance Sheet
December 31, 1999

| | | | | | |
|---|---|---|---|---|---|
| 1 | Assest | | | | 1 |
| 2 | | | | | 2 |
| 3 | | | | | 3 |
| 4 | | | | | 4 |
| 5 | | | | | 5 |
| 6 | | | | | 6 |
| 7 | | | | | 7 |
| 8 | | | | | 8 |
| 9 | | | | | 9 |
| 10 | | | | | 10 |
| 11 | | | | | 11 |
| 12 | | | | | 12 |
| 13 | | | | | 13 |
| 14 | | | | | 14 |
| 15 | | | | | 15 |
| 16 | | | | | 16 |
| 17 | Liabilities and Owner's Equity | | | | 17 |
| 18 | | | | | 18 |
| 19 | | | | | 19 |
| 20 | | | | | 20 |
| 21 | | | | | 21 |
| 22 | | | | | 22 |
| 23 | | | | | 23 |
| 24 | | | | | 24 |
| 25 | | | | | 25 |
| 26 | | | | | 26 |
| 27 | | | | | 27 |
| 28 | | | | | 28 |
| 29 | | | | | 29 |
| 30 | | | | | 30 |

Name

Section

Date

**Problem 5-4A Concluded**

**Rowbuck Department Store**

(b) and (c)

General Journal

| Date | Account Titles and Explanation | Ref. | Debit | Credit |
|---|---|---|---|---|
| (b) | Adjusting Entries | | | |
| | | | | |
| | | | | |
| | | | | |
| | | | | |
| | | | | |
| | | | | |
| | | | | |
| | | | | |
| | | | | |
| | | | | |
| | | | | |
| | | | | |
| | | | | |
| | | | | |
| | | | | |
| | | | | |
| (d) | Closing Entries | | | |
| | | | | |
| | | | | |
| | | | | |
| | | | | |
| | | | | |
| | | | | |
| | | | | |
| | | | | |
| | | | | |
| | | | | |
| | | | | |
| | | | | |
| | | | | |
| | | | | |
| | | | | |
| | | | | |
| | | | | |
| | | | | |
| | | | | |
| | | | | |
| | | | | |
| | | | | |

Name Problem 5-5A

Section

Date Chi Chi's Pro Shop

(a) General Journal

| Date | Account Titles and Explanation | Ref. | Debit | Credit |
|---|---|---|---|---|

Name

Section

Date



(b)

Cash — No. 101

| Date | Explanation | Ref. | Debit | Credit | Balance |
|---|---|---|---|---|---|
| | | | | | |
| | | | | | |
| | | | | | |
| | | | | | |
| | | | | | |
| | | | | | |

Accounts Receivable — No. 112

| Date | Explanation | Ref. | Debit | Credit | Balance |
|---|---|---|---|---|---|
| | | | | | |
| | | | | | |
| | | | | | |
| | | | | | |
| | | | | | |

Merchandise Inventory — No. 120

| Date | Explanation | Ref. | Debit | Credit | Balance |
|---|---|---|---|---|---|
| | | | | | |
| | | | | | |
| | | | | | |
| | | | | | |
| | | | | | |
| | | | | | |
| | | | | | |
| | | | | | |
| | | | | | |
| | | | | | |
| | | | | | |
| | | | | | |

Accounts Payable — No. 201

| Date | Explanation | Ref. | Debit | Credit | Balance |
|---|---|---|---|---|---|
| | | | | | |
| | | | | | |
| | | | | | |
| | | | | | |
| | | | | | |
| | | | | | |
| | | | | | |

(b) (Continued)

G. Garcia, Capital — No. 301

| Date | Explanation | Ref. | Debit | Credit | Balance |
|---|---|---|---|---|---|
| | | | | | |
| | | | | | |

Sales — No. 401

| Date | Explanation | Ref. | Debit | Credit | Balance |
|---|---|---|---|---|---|
| | | | | | |
| | | | | | |
| | | | | | |

Sales Returns and Allowances — No. 412

| Date | Explanation | Ref. | Debit | Credit | Balance |
|---|---|---|---|---|---|
| | | | | | |
| | | | | | |

Cost of Goods Sold — No. 505

| Date | Explanation | Ref. | Debit | Credit | Balance |
|---|---|---|---|---|---|
| | | | | | |
| | | | | | |
| | | | | | |

(c)

CHI CHI'S PRO SHOP
Trial Balance
April 30, 1999

| | | Debit | Credit | |
|---|---|---|---|---|
| 1 | | | | 1 |
| 2 | | | | 2 |
| 3 | | | | 3 |
| 4 | | | | 4 |
| 5 | | | | 5 |
| 6 | | | | 6 |
| 7 | | | | 7 |
| 8 | | | | 8 |
| 9 | | | | 9 |
| 10 | | | | 10 |
| 11 | | | | 11 |
| 12 | | | | 12 |

Name

Section

Date

**Problem 5-1B**

**Maggie Zine Distributing Company**

(a)

General Journal

| Date | Account Titles and Explanation | Ref. | Debit | Credit |
|---|---|---|---|---|

Name
Section
Date

**Problem 5-1B Continued**

**Maggie Zine Distributing Company**

(a) (Continued)

General Journal

| | Date | Account Titles and Explanation | Ref. | Debit | Credit | |
|---|---|---|---|---|---|---|
| 1 | | | | | | 1 |
| 2 | | | | | | 2 |
| 3 | | | | | | 3 |
| 4 | | | | | | 4 |
| 5 | | | | | | 5 |
| 6 | | | | | | 6 |
| 7 | | | | | | 7 |
| 8 | | | | | | 8 |
| 9 | | | | | | 9 |
| 10 | | | | | | 10 |
| 11 | | | | | | 11 |
| 12 | | | | | | 12 |
| 13 | | | | | | 13 |
| 14 | | | | | | 14 |
| 15 | | | | | | 15 |
| 16 | | | | | | 16 |
| 17 | | | | | | 17 |
| 18 | | | | | | 18 |

(b)

Cash No. 101

| Date | Explanation | Ref. | Debit | Credit | Balance |
|---|---|---|---|---|---|
| | | | | | |
| | | | | | |
| | | | | | |
| | | | | | |
| | | | | | |
| | | | | | |
| | | | | | |
| | | | | | |
| | | | | | |
| | | | | | |
| | | | | | |
| | | | | | |

Accounts Receivable No. 112

| Date | Explanation | Ref. | Debit | Credit | Balance |
|---|---|---|---|---|---|
| | | | | | |
| | | | | | |
| | | | | | |

(b) (Continued)

Merchandise Inventory — No. 120

| Date | Explanation | Ref. | Debit | Credit | Balance |
|---|---|---|---|---|---|
| | | | | | |
| | | | | | |
| | | | | | |
| | | | | | |
| | | | | | |
| | | | | | |
| | | | | | |
| | | | | | |
| | | | | | |
| | | | | | |
| | | | | | |
| | | | | | |
| | | | | | |
| | | | | | |

Accounts Payable — No. 201

| Date | Explanation | Ref. | Debit | Credit | Balance |
|---|---|---|---|---|---|
| | | | | | |
| | | | | | |
| | | | | | |
| | | | | | |
| | | | | | |
| | | | | | |

M. Zine, Capital — No. 301

| Date | Explanation | Ref. | Debit | Credit | Balance |
|---|---|---|---|---|---|
| | | | | | |
| | | | | | |

Sales — No. 401

| Date | Explanation | Ref. | Debit | Credit | Balance |
|---|---|---|---|---|---|
| | | | | | |
| | | | | | |
| | | | | | |
| | | | | | |

Name

Section

Date

**Maggie Zine Distributing Company**

(b) (Continued)

Sales Returns and Allowances — No. 412

| Date | Explanation | Ref. | Debit | Credit | Balance |
|---|---|---|---|---|---|
| | | | | | |
| | | | | | |

Sales Discounts — No. 414

| Date | Explanation | Ref. | Debit | Credit | Balance |
|---|---|---|---|---|---|
| | | | | | |
| | | | | | |

Cost of Goods Sold — No. 505

| Date | Explanation | Ref. | Debit | Credit | Balance |
|---|---|---|---|---|---|
| | | | | | |
| | | | | | |
| | | | | | |
| | | | | | |
| | | | | | |

Freight-out — No. 644

| Date | Explanation | Ref. | Debit | Credit | Balance |
|---|---|---|---|---|---|
| | | | | | |
| | | | | | |

(c)

MAGGIE ZINE DISTRIBUTING COMPANY

Income Statement (Partial)

For the Month Ended April 30, 1999

Name

Section

Date

**Problem 5-2B**

**Tom E. Hawks Auto Sales**

General Journal

| Date | Account Titles and Explanation | Ref. | Debit | Credit |
|---|---|---|---|---|

Name

Section

Date

**Problem 5-3B Continued**

**Cal. A. Fornia Fashion Center**

Additional working papers for this problem are at the back of this book.

(b)

CAL. A. FORNIA FASHION CENTER

Income Statement

For the Year Ended December 31, 1999

Name

Section

Date

**Problem 5-3B Continued**

**Cal. A. Fornia Fashion Center**

(b) (Continued)

CAL. A. FORNIA FASHION CENTER

Owner's Equity Statement

For the Year Ended November 30, 1999

| | |
|---|---|
| | |
| | |
| | |
| | |
| | |
| | |

CAL. A. FORNIA FASHION CENTER

Balance Sheet

December 31, 1999

| | | | |
|---|---|---|---|
| Assest | | | |
| | | | |
| | | | |
| | | | |
| | | | |
| | | | |
| | | | |
| | | | |
| | | | |
| | | | |
| | | | |
| | | | |
| | | | |
| | | | |
| | | | |
| | | | |
| Liabilities and Owner's Equity | | | |
| | | | |
| | | | |
| | | | |
| | | | |
| | | | |
| | | | |
| | | | |
| | | | |
| | | | |
| | | | |
| | | | |
| | | | |
| | | | |

Name

Section

Date

**Problem 5-3B Continued**

**Cal. A. Fornia Fashion Center**

(c) and (d)

General Journal

| Date | Account Titles and Explanation | Ref. | Debit | Credit |
|---|---|---|---|---|
| (c) | Adjustment Entries | | | |
| | | | | |
| | | | | |
| | | | | |
| | | | | |
| | | | | |
| | | | | |
| | | | | |
| | | | | |
| | | | | |
| | | | | |
| | | | | |
| | | | | |
| | | | | |
| | | | | |
| | | | | |
| | | | | |
| | | | | |
| | | | | |
| | | | | |
| (d) | Closing Entries | | | |
| | | | | |
| | | | | |
| | | | | |
| | | | | |
| | | | | |
| | | | | |
| | | | | |
| | | | | |
| | | | | |
| | | | | |
| | | | | |
| | | | | |
| | | | | |
| | | | | |
| | | | | |
| | | | | |
| | | | | |
| | | | | |
| | | | | |

Name

Section

Date





(d) (Continued)

General Journal

| | Date | Account Titles and Explanation | Ref. | Debit | Credit | |
|---|---|---|---|---|---|---|
| 1 | | | | | | 1 |
| 2 | | | | | | 2 |
| 3 | | | | | | 3 |
| 4 | | | | | | 4 |
| 5 | | | | | | 5 |
| 6 | | | | | | 6 |
| 7 | | | | | | 7 |
| 8 | | | | | | 8 |
| 9 | | | | | | 9 |
| 10 | | | | | | 10 |
| 11 | | | | | | 11 |
| 12 | | | | | | 12 |
| 13 | | | | | | 13 |
| 14 | | | | | | 14 |
| 15 | | | | | | 15 |

(e)

CAL. A. FORNIA FASHION CENTER
Post-Closing Trial Balance
November 30, 1999

| | | Debit | Credit | |
|---|---|---|---|---|
| 1 | | | | 1 |
| 2 | | | | 2 |
| 3 | | | | 3 |
| 4 | | | | 4 |
| 5 | | | | 5 |
| 6 | | | | 6 |
| 7 | | | | 7 |
| 8 | | | | 8 |
| 9 | | | | 9 |
| 10 | | | | 10 |
| 11 | | | | 11 |
| 12 | | | | 12 |
| 13 | | | | 13 |
| 14 | | | | 14 |
| 15 | | | | 15 |
| 16 | | | | 16 |
| 17 | | | | 17 |

Name

Section

Date

**Problem 5-4B**

**Al Falfa Department Store**

(a)

AL FALFA DEPARTMENT STORE

Income Statement

For the Year Ended November 30, 1999

Name
Section
Date

**Problem 5-4B Continued**

**Al Falfa Department Store**

(a) (Continued)

AL FALFA DEPARTMENT STORE
Income Statement (Continued)
For the Year Ended December 31, 1999

| | | | |
|---|---|---|---|
| | | | |
| | | | |
| | | | |
| | | | |

AL FALFA DEPARTMENT STORE
Owner's Equity Statement
For the Year Ended December 31, 1999

| | |
|---|---|
| | |
| | |
| | |
| | |
| | |
| | |

(b)

General Journal

| Date | Account Titles and Explanation | Ref. | Debit | Credit |
|---|---|---|---|---|
| | Adjustment Entries | | | |
| | | | | |
| | | | | |
| | | | | |
| | | | | |
| | | | | |
| | | | | |
| | | | | |
| | | | | |
| | | | | |
| | | | | |
| | | | | |
| | | | | |
| | | | | |
| | | | | |
| | | | | |
| | | | | |
| | | | | |
| | | | | |
| | | | | |

(a) (Continued)

AL FALFA DEPARTMENT STORE
Balance Sheet
December 31, 1999

Assets

Liabilities and Owner's Equity

Name

Section

Date

**Problem 5-4B Conclude**

**Al Falfa Department Store**

(c) General Journal

| Date | Account Titles and Explanation | Ref. | Debit | Credit |
|---|---|---|---|---|
| | Closing Entries | | | |

 

Name

Section

Date

**Problem 5-5B**

**B. J.'s Tennis Shop**

(a) General Journal J1

| Date | Account Titles and Explanation | Ref. | Debit | Credit |
|---|---|---|---|---|

Name

Section

Date

**Problem 5-5B Continued**

**B. J.'s Tennis Shop**

(a) (Continued)

General Journal

| Date | Account Titles and Explanation | Ref. | Debit | Credit |
|---|---|---|---|---|
| | | | | |

(b)

Cash — No. 101

| Date | Explanation | Ref. | Debit | Credit | Balance |
|---|---|---|---|---|---|
| | | | | | |

Accounts Receivable — No. 112

| Date | Explanation | Ref. | Debit | Credit | Balance |
|---|---|---|---|---|---|
| | | | | | |

Name | **Problem 5-5B Continued**

Section

Date | **B. J.'s Tennis Shop**

(b) (Continued)

Merchandise Inventory — No. 120

| Date | Explanation | Ref. | Debit | Credit | Balance |
|---|---|---|---|---|---|
| | | | | | |
| | | | | | |
| | | | | | |
| | | | | | |
| | | | | | |
| | | | | | |
| | | | | | |
| | | | | | |
| | | | | | |
| | | | | | |
| | | | | | |
| | | | | | |
| | | | | | |

Accounts Payable — No. 201

| Date | Explanation | Ref. | Debit | Credit | Balance |
|---|---|---|---|---|---|
| | | | | | |
| | | | | | |
| | | | | | |
| | | | | | |
| | | | | | |
| | | | | | |

B. J. Evans, Capital — No. 301

| Date | Explanation | Ref. | Debit | Credit | Balance |
|---|---|---|---|---|---|
| | | | | | |
| | | | | | |

Sales — No. 401

| Date | Explanation | Ref. | Debit | Credit | Balance |
|---|---|---|---|---|---|
| | | | | | |
| | | | | | |
| | | | | | |

Sales Returns and Allowances — No. 412

| Date | Explanation | Ref. | Debit | Credit | Balance |
|---|---|---|---|---|---|
| | | | | | |
| | | | | | |

(b) (Continued)

Cost of Goods Sold

No. 505

| Date | Explanation | Ref. | Debit | Credit | Balance |
|---|---|---|---|---|---|
| | | | | | |
| | | | | | |
| | | | | | |

(c)

B. J.'S TENNIS SHOP
Trial Balance
April 30, 1999

| | | Debit | Credit | |
|---|---|---|---|---|
| 1 | | | | 1 |
| 2 | | | | 2 |
| 3 | | | | 3 |
| 4 | | | | 4 |
| 5 | | | | 5 |
| 6 | | | | 6 |
| 7 | | | | 7 |
| 8 | | | | 8 |
| 9 | | | | 9 |
| 10 | | | | 10 |
| 11 | | | | 11 |
| 12 | | | | 12 |
| 13 | | | | 13 |
| 14 | | | | 14 |

Name
Section
Date



**Kellogg Company**

(a) (1) Percentage change in sales —

1996:

1997:

(2) Percentage change in net income —

1996:

1997:

(b) Gross profit rate —

1995:

1996:

1997:

(c) Percentage of net income to sales —

1995:

1996:

1997:

Name

Section

Date



| (a) | Kellogg | General Mills |
|---|---|---|
| (1) 1997 Gross profit | | |
| (2) 1997 Gross profit rate | | |
| (3) 1997 Operating income | | |
| (4) Percentage change in operating income, 1990 to 1997 | | |

(b)

 

Name

Section

Date

McDonnell Douglas

(a)

(b)

(c)

Name

Section

Date

(a) (1)

FEDCO DEPARTMENT STORE
Income Statement
For the Month Ended December 31, 1999

(2)

FEDCO DEPARTMENT STORE
Income Statement
For the Month Ended December 31, 1999

Name

Section

Date



(b)

(c)

FEDCO DEPARTMENT STORE
Income Statement
For the Year Ended December 31, 1999

Name

Section

Date



**REAL-WORLD FOCUS** A. L. Laboratories

(a)

(b)

(c)

**ETHICS CASE** Yorkshire Stores

(a)

(b)

Name

Section

Date



(c)

Name

Section

Date



| Date | Explanation | Ref. | Debit | Credit | Balance |
|---|---|---|---|---|---|
| | | | | | |
| | | | | | |
| | | | | | |

| Date | Explanation | Ref. | Debit | Credit | Balance |
|---|---|---|---|---|---|
| | | | | | |
| | | | | | |
| | | | | | |

| Date | Explanation | Ref. | Debit | Credit | Balance |
|---|---|---|---|---|---|
| | | | | | |
| | | | | | |
| | | | | | |

| Date | Explanation | Ref. | Debit | Credit | Balance |
|---|---|---|---|---|---|
| | | | | | |
| | | | | | |
| | | | | | |

Name
Section
Date

Name

Section

Date

Name

Section

Date

**Exercises 6-1 to 6-2**

**#1** (a)

(b)

(c)

(d)

**#2**

Name **Exercise 6-3**

Section

Date **Cremer Company**

(a) and (b)

*General Ledger*

Accounts Receivable

| Date | Explanation | Ref. | Debit | Credit | Balance |
|---|---|---|---|---|---|
| | | | | | |
| | | | | | |
| | | | | | |
| | | | | | |
| | | | | | |

*Accounts Receivable Subsidiary Ledger*

Alou

| Date | Explanation | Ref. | Debit | Credit | Balance |
|---|---|---|---|---|---|
| | | | | | |
| | | | | | |
| | | | | | |
| | | | | | |

Farr

| Date | Explanation | Ref. | Debit | Credit | Balance |
|---|---|---|---|---|---|
| | | | | | |
| | | | | | |
| | | | | | |

George

| Date | Explanation | Ref. | Debit | Credit | Balance |
|---|---|---|---|---|---|
| | | | | | |
| | | | | | |
| | | | | | |

Keaton

| Date | Explanation | Ref. | Debit | Credit | Balance |
|---|---|---|---|---|---|
| | | | | | |
| | | | | | |
| | | | | | |
| | | | | | |

Skiles

| Date | Explanation | Ref. | Debit | Credit | Balance |
|---|---|---|---|---|---|
| | | | | | |
| | | | | | |
| | | | | | |
| | | | | | |
| | | | | | |

Name

Section

Date

**Exercise 6-3 Concluded to Exercise 6-4**

**#3** (c)

CREMER COMPANY
Schedule of Customers
As of September 30, 1999

| | | |
|---|---|---|
| 1 | | 1 |
| 2 | | 2 |
| 3 | | 3 |
| 4 | | 4 |
| 5 | | 5 |
| 6 | | 6 |
| 7 | | 7 |
| 8 | | 8 |
| 9 | | 9 |
| 10 | | 10 |
| 11 | | 11 |
| 12 | | 12 |

**#4**

HARRIS COMPANY
Sales Journal

S1

| Date | Account Debited | Invoice No. | Ref. | Accounts Receiv. Dr. Sales Cr. | COGS Dr. Merchan. Inventory Cr. |
|---|---|---|---|---|---|
| | | | | | |
| | | | | | |
| | | | | | |
| | | | | | |
| | | | | | |

HARRIS COMPANY
Purchases Journal

P1

| Date | Account Credited | Terms | Ref. | Merchandise Inventory (Dr.) Acc. Pay. (Cr.) |
|---|---|---|---|---|
| | | | | |
| | | | | |
| | | | | |
| | | | | |
| | | | | |

Name

Section

Date



**#5**

BRIGGS CO.

Cash Receipts Journal

CR1

| Date | Account Credited | Ref. | Cash Dr. | Sales Discounts Dr. | Accounts Receivable Cr. | Sales Cr. | Other Accounts Cr. | COGS Dr. Inventory Cr. |
|---|---|---|---|---|---|---|---|---|
| | | | | | | | | |
| | | | | | | | | |
| | | | | | | | | |
| | | | | | | | | |
| | | | | | | | | |
| | | | | | | | | |

BRIGGS CO.

Cash Payments Journal

CP1

| Date | Account Debited | Ref. | Other Accounts Dr. | Accounts Payable Dr. | Cash Cr. |
|---|---|---|---|---|---|
| | | | | | |
| | | | | | |
| | | | | | |
| | | | | | |
| | | | | | |
| | | | | | |

**#6**

| | (a) Journal | (b) Journal Columns | |
|---|---|---|---|
| 1 | | | 1 |
| 2 | | | 2 |
| 3 | | | 3 |
| 4 | | | 4 |
| 5 | | | 5 |
| 6 | | | 6 |
| 7 | | | 7 |
| 8 | | | 8 |
| 9 | | | 9 |
| 10 | | | 10 |
| 11 | | | 11 |
| 12 | | | 12 |
| 13 | | | 13 |
| 14 | | | 14 |
| 15 | | | 15 |

Name

Section

Date

**Exercise 6-7**

**Warner Company**

(a)

(b)

Name                                                                                     **Exercises 6-8 to 6-9**

Section

Date

**#8**

**#9** (a)

(b)

Name

Section

Date

**Exercises 6-10 to 6-11**

**#10**

MOYER COMPANY

(a) Purchases Journal P1

| Date | Account Credited | Terms | Ref. | Merchandise Inventory (Dr.) Acc. Pay. (Cr.) |
|---|---|---|---|---|
| | | | | |
| | | | | |
| | | | | |
| | | | | |
| | | | | |
| | | | | |
| | | | | |
| | | | | |

(b) General Journal

| | Date | Account Titles and Explanation | Ref. | Debit | Credit | |
|---|---|---|---|---|---|---|
| 1 | | | | | | 1 |
| 2 | | | | | | 2 |
| 3 | | | | | | 3 |
| 4 | | | | | | 4 |
| 5 | | | | | | 5 |
| 6 | | | | | | 6 |
| 7 | | | | | | 7 |
| 8 | | | | | | 8 |
| 9 | | | | | | 9 |
| 10 | | | | | | 10 |
| 11 | | | | | | 11 |
| 12 | | | | | | 12 |
| 13 | | | | | | 13 |
| 14 | | | | | | 14 |
| 15 | | | | | | 15 |

**#11**

| | | | | |
|---|---|---|---|---|
| 1 | | | | 1 |
| 2 | | | | 2 |
| 3 | | | | 3 |
| 4 | | | | 4 |
| 5 | | | | 5 |
| 6 | | | | 6 |

Name | Problem 6-1A
Section
Date | **Koslo Company**

(a)

KOSLO COMPANY
Cash Receipts Journal

CR1

| Date | Account Credited | Ref. | Cash Dr. | Sales Discounts Dr. | Accounts Receivable Cr. | Sales Cr. | Other Accounts Cr. | COGS Dr. Inventory Cr. |
|---|---|---|---|---|---|---|---|---|

(b)

*General Ledger*
Accounts Receivable

No.112

| Date | Explanation | Ref. | Debit | Credit | Balance |
|---|---|---|---|---|---|

Name

Section

Date



(b) (Continued) *Accounts Receivable Subsidiary Ledger*

Ben & Son

| Date | Explanation | Ref. | Debit | Credit | Balance |
|---|---|---|---|---|---|
| | | | | | |
| | | | | | |
| | | | | | |

Ellis Co.

| Date | Explanation | Ref. | Debit | Credit | Balance |
|---|---|---|---|---|---|
| | | | | | |
| | | | | | |
| | | | | | |

Gant Bros.

| Date | Explanation | Ref. | Debit | Credit | Balance |
|---|---|---|---|---|---|
| | | | | | |
| | | | | | |
| | | | | | |

Meija Co.

| Date | Explanation | Ref. | Debit | Credit | Balance |
|---|---|---|---|---|---|
| | | | | | |
| | | | | | |
| | | | | | |

(c)

Accounts receivable balance:

Sum of subsidiary accounts:

Name

Section

Date

**Problem 6-2A**

**Cline Company**

CLINE COMPANY

(a) Cash Payments Journal CP1

| Date | Ck. No. | Account Debited | Ref. | Other Accounts Dr. | Accounts Payable Dr. | Merchan. Inventory Cr. | Cash Cr. |
|---|---|---|---|---|---|---|---|
| | | | | | | | |
| | | | | | | | |
| | | | | | | | |
| | | | | | | | |
| | | | | | | | |
| | | | | | | | |
| | | | | | | | |
| | | | | | | | |
| | | | | | | | |
| | | | | | | | |
| | | | | | | | |
| | | | | | | | |
| | | | | | | | |
| | | | | | | | |
| | | | | | | | |
| | | | | | | | |
| | | | | | | | |
| | | | | | | | |
| | | | | | | | |
| | | | | | | | |
| | | | | | | | |
| | | | | | | | |
| | | | | | | | |
| | | | | | | | |
| | | | | | | | |

(b) *General Ledger*

Accounts Payable No. 201

| Date | Explanation | Ref. | Debit | Credit | Balance |
|---|---|---|---|---|---|
| | | | | | |
| | | | | | |
| | | | | | |
| | | | | | |

Name
Section
Date

**Problem 6-2A Concluded**

**Cline Company**

(b) (Continued)

*Accounts Payable Subsidiary Ledger*

S. Haley & Co.

| Date | Explanation | Ref. | Debit | Credit | Balance |
|---|---|---|---|---|---|
| | | | | | |
| | | | | | |
| | | | | | |

C. King

| Date | Explanation | Ref. | Debit | Credit | Balance |
|---|---|---|---|---|---|
| | | | | | |
| | | | | | |
| | | | | | |

W. Ortega

| Date | Explanation | Ref. | Debit | Credit | Balance |
|---|---|---|---|---|---|
| | | | | | |
| | | | | | |
| | | | | | |

Welch Bros.

| Date | Explanation | Ref. | Debit | Credit | Balance |
|---|---|---|---|---|---|
| | | | | | |
| | | | | | |
| | | | | | |

(c)

| | | |
|---|---|---|
| 1 | Accounts payable balance: | 1 |
| 2 | | 2 |
| 3 | | 3 |
| 4 | Sum of subsidiary accounts: | 4 |
| 5 | | 5 |
| 6 | | 6 |
| 7 | | 7 |
| 8 | | 8 |
| 9 | | 9 |
| 10 | | 10 |

Name | **Problem 6-3A**

Section

Date | **Pagnozzi Company**

PAGNOZZI COMPANY
Purchases Journal

(a) P1

| Date | Account Credited (Debited) | Terms | Ref. | Other Accounts Dr. | Merchan. Inventory Dr. | Accounts Payable Cr. |
|---|---|---|---|---|---|---|

PAGNOZZI COMPANY
Sales Journal

S1

| Date | Account Debited | Invoice No. | Ref. | Accounts Receiv. Dr. Sales Cr. | COGS Dr. Merchandise Inventory Cr. |
|---|---|---|---|---|---|

Name

Section

Date



(a) (Continued)

General Journal

| | Date | Account Titles and Explanation | Ref. | Debit | Credit | |
|---|---|---|---|---|---|---|
| 1 | | | | | | 1 |
| 2 | | | | | | 2 |
| 3 | | | | | | 3 |
| 4 | | | | | | 4 |
| 5 | | | | | | 5 |
| 6 | | | | | | 6 |
| 7 | | | | | | 7 |
| 8 | | | | | | 8 |
| 9 | | | | | | 9 |
| 10 | | | | | | 10 |
| 11 | | | | | | 11 |
| 12 | | | | | | 12 |
| 13 | | | | | | 13 |
| 14 | | | | | | 14 |
| 15 | | | | | | 15 |
| 16 | | | | | | 16 |
| 17 | | | | | | 17 |
| 18 | | | | | | 18 |

(b)

*General Ledger*

Accounts Receivable

No. 112

| Date | Explanation | Ref. | Debit | Credit | Balance |
|---|---|---|---|---|---|
| | | | | | |
| | | | | | |
| | | | | | |
| | | | | | |

Merchandise Inventory

No. 120

| Date | Explanation | Ref. | Debit | Credit | Balance |
|---|---|---|---|---|---|
| | | | | | |
| | | | | | |
| | | | | | |
| | | | | | |
| | | | | | |
| | | | | | |
| | | | | | |
| | | | | | |

(b) (Continued)

Supplies — No. 126

| Date | Explanation | Ref. | Debit | Credit | Balance |
|---|---|---|---|---|---|
| | | | | | |
| | | | | | |
| | | | | | |

Equipment — No. 157

| Date | Explanation | Ref. | Debit | Credit | Balance |
|---|---|---|---|---|---|
| | | | | | |
| | | | | | |

Accounts Payable — No. 201

| Date | Explanation | Ref. | Debit | Credit | Balance |
|---|---|---|---|---|---|
| | | | | | |
| | | | | | |
| | | | | | |
| | | | | | |
| | | | | | |

Sales — No. 401

| Date | Explanation | Ref. | Debit | Credit | Balance |
|---|---|---|---|---|---|
| | | | | | |
| | | | | | |

Sales Returns and Allowances — No. 412

| Date | Explanation | Ref. | Debit | Credit | Balance |
|---|---|---|---|---|---|
| | | | | | |
| | | | | | |

Name
Section
Date

**Problem 6-3A Continued**

**Pagnozzi Company**

(b) (Continued)

Cost of Goods Sold — No. 505

| Date | Explanation | Ref. | Debit | Credit | Balance |
| --- | --- | --- | --- | --- | --- |
| | | | | | |
| | | | | | |
| | | | | | |

Advertising Expense — No. 610

| Date | Explanation | Ref. | Debit | Credit | Balance |
| --- | --- | --- | --- | --- | --- |
| | | | | | |
| | | | | | |

*Accounts Receivable Subsidiary Ledger*

Potts Company

| Date | Explanation | Ref. | Debit | Credit | Balance |
| --- | --- | --- | --- | --- | --- |
| | | | | | |
| | | | | | |

Hogan Bros.

| Date | Explanation | Ref. | Debit | Credit | Balance |
| --- | --- | --- | --- | --- | --- |
| | | | | | |
| | | | | | |
| | | | | | |

Nance Company

| Date | Explanation | Ref. | Debit | Credit | Balance |
| --- | --- | --- | --- | --- | --- |
| | | | | | |
| | | | | | |
| | | | | | |
| | | | | | |

Name | Problem 6-3A Continued
Section
Date | Pagnozzi Company

(b) (Continued)

*Accounts Payable Subsidiary Ledger*

Abel Freight

| Date | Explanation | Ref. | Debit | Credit | Balance |
|---|---|---|---|---|---|
| | | | | | |
| | | | | | |
| | | | | | |

Vena Company

| Date | Explanation | Ref. | Debit | Credit | Balance |
|---|---|---|---|---|---|
| | | | | | |
| | | | | | |
| | | | | | |
| | | | | | |

Eaton Supply

| Date | Explanation | Ref. | Debit | Credit | Balance |
|---|---|---|---|---|---|
| | | | | | |
| | | | | | |
| | | | | | |
| | | | | | |

Gore Company

| Date | Explanation | Ref. | Debit | Credit | Balance |
|---|---|---|---|---|---|
| | | | | | |
| | | | | | |
| | | | | | |

Deleon Company

| Date | Explanation | Ref. | Debit | Credit | Balance |
|---|---|---|---|---|---|
| | | | | | |
| | | | | | |
| | | | | | |

Beck Advertising

| Date | Explanation | Ref. | Debit | Credit | Balance |
|---|---|---|---|---|---|
| | | | | | |
| | | | | | |
| | | | | | |

Name
Section
Date

**Problem 6-3A Concluded**

**Pagnozzi Company**

(c)

Accounts receivable balance:

Sum of subsidiary accounts:

Accounts payable balance:

Sum of subsidiary accounts:

Name **Problem 6-4A**

Section

Date **Santos Company**

(a), (b) and (c)

SANTOS COMPANY

Sales Journal S1

| Date | Account Debited | Invoice No. | Ref. | Accounts Receiv. Dr. Sales Cr. | COGS Dr. Merchan. Inventory Cr. |
|---|---|---|---|---|---|
| | | | | | |
| | | | | | |
| | | | | | |
| | | | | | |
| | | | | | |
| | | | | | |
| | | | | | |
| | | | | | |
| | | | | | |
| | | | | | |

SANTOS COMPANY

Purchases Journal P1

| Date | Account Credited | Terms | Ref. | Merchandise Inventory (Dr.) Acc. Pay. (Cr.) |
|---|---|---|---|---|
| | | | | |
| | | | | |
| | | | | |
| | | | | |
| | | | | |
| | | | | |
| | | | | |
| | | | | |
| | | | | |
| | | | | |

General Journal G1

| Date | Account Titles and Explanation | Ref. | Debit | Credit |
|---|---|---|---|---|
| | | | | |
| | | | | |
| | | | | |
| | | | | |
| | | | | |
| | | | | |
| | | | | |
| | | | | |

Name

Section

Date



(a), (b), and (c) (Continued)

SANTOS COMPANY
Cash Receipts Journal

CR1

| Date | Account Credited | Ref. | Cash Dr. | Sales Discounts Dr. | Accounts Receivable Cr. | Sales Cr. | Other Accounts Cr. | COGS Dr. Inventory Cr. |
|---|---|---|---|---|---|---|---|---|
| | | | | | | | | |
| | | | | | | | | |
| | | | | | | | | |
| | | | | | | | | |
| | | | | | | | | |
| | | | | | | | | |
| | | | | | | | | |
| | | | | | | | | |
| | | | | | | | | |
| | | | | | | | | |
| | | | | | | | | |
| | | | | | | | | |
| | | | | | | | | |
| | | | | | | | | |
| | | | | | | | | |

SANTOS COMPANY
Cash Payments Journal

CP1

| Date | Account Debited | Ref. | Other Accounts Dr. | Accounts Payable Dr. | Merchan. Inventory Cr. | Cash Cr. |
|---|---|---|---|---|---|---|
| | | | | | | |
| | | | | | | |
| | | | | | | |
| | | | | | | |
| | | | | | | |
| | | | | | | |
| | | | | | | |
| | | | | | | |
| | | | | | | |
| | | | | | | |
| | | | | | | |
| | | | | | | |
| | | | | | | |
| | | | | | | |
| | | | | | | |

Name | **Problem 6-5A**

Section

Date | **Tino Co.**

(a), (d) and (g)

*General Ledger*

Cash — No. 101

| Date | Explanation | Ref. | Debit | Credit | Balance |
|---|---|---|---|---|---|
| | | | | | |
| | | | | | |
| | | | | | |

Accounts Receivable — No. 112

| Date | Explanation | Ref. | Debit | Credit | Balance |
|---|---|---|---|---|---|
| | | | | | |
| | | | | | |
| | | | | | |

Merchandise Inventory — No. 120

| Date | Explanation | Ref. | Debit | Credit | Balance |
|---|---|---|---|---|---|
| | | | | | |
| | | | | | |
| | | | | | |
| | | | | | |
| | | | | | |

Supplies — No. 126

| Date | Explanation | Ref. | Debit | Credit | Balance |
|---|---|---|---|---|---|
| | | | | | |
| | | | | | |
| | | | | | |

Equipment — No. 157

| Date | Explanation | Ref. | Debit | Credit | Balance |
|---|---|---|---|---|---|
| | | | | | |
| | | | | | |

Accumulated Depreciation — Equipment — No. 158

| Date | Explanation | Ref. | Debit | Credit | Balance |
|---|---|---|---|---|---|
| | | | | | |
| | | | | | |

Name
Section
Date

**Problem 6-5A Continued**

**Tino Co.**

(a), (d) and (g) (Continued)

Accounts Payable — No. 201

| Date | Explanation | Ref. | Debit | Credit | Balance |
| --- | --- | --- | --- | --- | --- |
| | | | | | |
| | | | | | |
| | | | | | |

J. Tino, Capital — No. 301

| Date | Explanation | Ref. | Debit | Credit | Balance |
| --- | --- | --- | --- | --- | --- |
| | | | | | |
| | | | | | |

J. Tino, Drawing — No. 306

| Date | Explanation | Ref. | Debit | Credit | Balance |
| --- | --- | --- | --- | --- | --- |
| | | | | | |
| | | | | | |

Sales — No. 401

| Date | Explanation | Ref. | Debit | Credit | Balance |
| --- | --- | --- | --- | --- | --- |
| | | | | | |
| | | | | | |
| | | | | | |

Sales Discounts — No. 414

| Date | Explanation | Ref. | Debit | Credit | Balance |
| --- | --- | --- | --- | --- | --- |
| | | | | | |
| | | | | | |

Cost of Goods Sold — No. 505

| Date | Explanation | Ref. | Debit | Credit | Balance |
| --- | --- | --- | --- | --- | --- |
| | | | | | |
| | | | | | |
| | | | | | |

(a), (d) and (g) (Continued)

Supplies Expense — No. 631

| Date | Explanation | Ref. | Debit | Credit | Balance |
|---|---|---|---|---|---|
| | | | | | |
| | | | | | |

Depreciation Expense — No. 711

| Date | Explanation | Ref. | Debit | Credit | Balance |
|---|---|---|---|---|---|
| | | | | | |
| | | | | | |

(b)

TINO CO.
Purchases Journal — P1

| Date | Account Credited | Terms | Ref. | Merchandise Inventory (Dr.) Acc. Pay. (Cr.) |
|---|---|---|---|---|
| | | | | |
| | | | | |
| | | | | |
| | | | | |
| | | | | |
| | | | | |
| | | | | |
| | | | | |
| | | | | |
| | | | | |
| | | | | |

TINO CO.
Cash Payments Journal — CP1

| Date | Account Debited | Ref. | Other Accounts Dr. | Accounts Payable Dr. | Merchan. Inventory Cr. | Cash Cr. |
|---|---|---|---|---|---|---|
| | | | | | | |
| | | | | | | |
| | | | | | | |
| | | | | | | |
| | | | | | | |
| | | | | | | |
| | | | | | | |
| | | | | | | |
| | | | | | | |
| | | | | | | |
| | | | | | | |

(c)

*Accounts Receivable Subsidiary Ledger*

D. Alco

| Date | Explanation | Ref. | Debit | Credit | Balance |
|---|---|---|---|---|---|
| | | | | | |
| | | | | | |
| | | | | | |

D. Casey

| Date | Explanation | Ref. | Debit | Credit | Balance |
|---|---|---|---|---|---|
| | | | | | |
| | | | | | |

P. Barber

| Date | Explanation | Ref. | Debit | Credit | Balance |
|---|---|---|---|---|---|
| | | | | | |
| | | | | | |
| | | | | | |

K. Dennis

| Date | Explanation | Ref. | Debit | Credit | Balance |
|---|---|---|---|---|---|
| | | | | | |
| | | | | | |

*Accounts Payable Subsidiary Ledger*

G. Azar

| Date | Explanation | Ref. | Debit | Credit | Balance |
|---|---|---|---|---|---|
| | | | | | |
| | | | | | |

J. Carson

| Date | Explanation | Ref. | Debit | Credit | Balance |
|---|---|---|---|---|---|
| | | | | | |
| | | | | | |
| | | | | | |

K. Cooper

| Date | Explanation | Ref. | Debit | Credit | Balance |
|---|---|---|---|---|---|
| | | | | | |
| | | | | | |
| | | | | | |

Name | Problem 6-5A Continued

Section

Date | Tino Co.

(c) (Continued)

M. Kim

| Date | Explanation | Ref. | Debit | Credit | Balance |
|---|---|---|---|---|---|
| | | | | | |
| | | | | | |
| | | | | | |

(e)

TINO CO.
Trial Balance
February 28, 1999

| | | Debit | Credit | |
|---|---|---|---|---|
| 1 | Cash | | | 1 |
| 2 | Accounts Receivable | | | 2 |
| 3 | Merchandise Inventory | | | 3 |
| 4 | Supplies | | | 4 |
| 5 | Equipment | | | 5 |
| 6 | Accounts Payable | | | 6 |
| 7 | J. Tino, Capital | | | 7 |
| 8 | J. Tino, Drawing | | | 8 |
| 9 | Sales | | | 9 |
| 10 | Sales Discounts | | | 10 |
| 11 | Cost of Goods Sold | | | 11 |
| 12 | | | | 12 |
| 13 | | | | 13 |

(f)

| | | | | |
|---|---|---|---|---|
| 1 | Accounts receivable control account: | | | 1 |
| 2 | | | | 2 |
| 3 | Accounts receivable subsidiary accounts: | | | 3 |
| 4 | | | | 4 |
| 5 | | | | 5 |
| 6 | | | | 6 |
| 7 | | | | 7 |
| 8 | Accounts payable control account: | | | 8 |
| 9 | | | | 9 |
| 10 | Accounts payable subsidiary accounts: | | | 10 |
| 11 | | | | 11 |
| 12 | | | | 12 |
| 13 | | | | 13 |

Name

Section

Date

**Problem 6-5A Concluded**

**Tino Co.**

(g) General Journal G1

| Date | Account Titles and Explanation | Ref. | Debit | Credit |
|---|---|---|---|---|
| | | | | |
| | | | | |
| | | | | |
| | | | | |
| | | | | |
| | | | | |
| | | | | |
| | | | | |
| | | | | |
| | | | | |

(h)

TINO CO.
Adjusted Trial Balance
February 28, 1999

| | Debit | Credit |
|---|---|---|
| Cash | | |
| Accounts Receivable | | |
| Merchandise Inventory | | |
| Supplies | | |
| Equipment | | |
| Accumulated Depreciation—Equipment | | |
| Accounts Payable | | |
| J. Tino, Capital | | |
| J. Tino, Drawing | | |
| Sales | | |
| Sales Discounts | | |
| Cost of Goods Sold | | |
| Supplies Expense | | |
| Depreciation Expense | | |
| | | |
| | | |
| | | |
| | | |
| | | |
| | | |

Name Problem 6-6A
Section
Date Gonzalez Co.

(b)

GONZALEZ CO.
Sales Journal S1

| Date | Account Debited | Invoice No. | Ref. | Accounts Receiv. Dr. Sales Cr. | COGS Dr. Merchan. Inventory Cr. |
|---|---|---|---|---|---|
| | | | | | |
| | | | | | |
| | | | | | |
| | | | | | |
| | | | | | |
| | | | | | |

GONZALEZ CO.
Purchases Journal P1

| Date | Account Credited | Terms | Ref. | Merchandise Inventory Dr. Acc. Pay. Cr. |
|---|---|---|---|---|
| | | | | |
| | | | | |
| | | | | |
| | | | | |
| | | | | |
| | | | | |

General Journal G1

| | Date | Account Titles and Explanation | Ref. | Debit | Credit | |
|---|---|---|---|---|---|---|
| 1 | | | | | | 1 |
| 2 | | | | | | 2 |
| 3 | | | | | | 3 |
| 4 | | | | | | 4 |
| 5 | | | | | | 5 |
| 6 | | | | | | 6 |
| 7 | | | | | | 7 |
| 8 | | | | | | 8 |
| 9 | | | | | | 9 |
| 10 | | | | | | 10 |
| 11 | | | | | | 11 |
| 12 | | | | | | 12 |
| 13 | | | | | | 13 |
| 14 | | | | | | 14 |
| 15 | | | | | | 15 |

(b) (Continued)

GONZALEZ CO.
Cash Receipts Journal

CR1

| Date | Account Credited | Ref. | Cash Dr. | Sales Discounts Dr. | Accounts Receivable Cr. | Sales Cr. | Other Accounts Cr. | COGS Dr. Inventory Cr. |
|---|---|---|---|---|---|---|---|---|
| | | | | | | | | |
| | | | | | | | | |
| | | | | | | | | |
| | | | | | | | | |
| | | | | | | | | |
| | | | | | | | | |
| | | | | | | | | |
| | | | | | | | | |
| | | | | | | | | |
| | | | | | | | | |
| | | | | | | | | |
| | | | | | | | | |
| | | | | | | | | |

GONZALEZ CO.
Cash Payments Journal

CP1

| Date | Account Debited | Ref. | Other Accounts Dr. | Accounts Payable Dr. | Merchan. Inventory Cr. | Cash Cr. |
|---|---|---|---|---|---|---|
| | | | | | | |
| | | | | | | |
| | | | | | | |
| | | | | | | |
| | | | | | | |
| | | | | | | |
| | | | | | | |
| | | | | | | |
| | | | | | | |
| | | | | | | |

(a) and (c)

*General Ledger*

Cash

No. 101

| Date | Explanation | Ref. | Debit | Credit | Balance |
|---|---|---|---|---|---|
| | | | | | |
| | | | | | |
| | | | | | |
| | | | | | |

Name

Section

Date

**Problem 6-6A Continued**

**Gonzalez Company**

(a) and (c)

Accounts Receivable — No. 112

| Date | Explanation | Ref. | Debit | Credit | Balance |
|---|---|---|---|---|---|
| | | | | | |
| | | | | | |
| | | | | | |
| | | | | | |
| | | | | | |

Notes Receivable — No. 115

| Date | Explanation | Ref. | Debit | Credit | Balance |
|---|---|---|---|---|---|
| | | | | | |
| | | | | | |
| | | | | | |

Merchandise Inventory — No. 120

| Date | Explanation | Ref. | Debit | Credit | Balance |
|---|---|---|---|---|---|
| | | | | | |
| | | | | | |
| | | | | | |
| | | | | | |
| | | | | | |
| | | | | | |
| | | | | | |
| | | | | | |

Equipment — No. 157

| Date | Explanation | Ref. | Debit | Credit | Balance |
|---|---|---|---|---|---|
| | | | | | |
| | | | | | |

Accumulated Depreciation — Equipment — No. 158

| Date | Explanation | Ref. | Debit | Credit | Balance |
|---|---|---|---|---|---|
| | | | | | |
| | | | | | |

Notes Payable — No. 200

| Date | Explanation | Ref. | Debit | Credit | Balance |
|---|---|---|---|---|---|
| | | | | | |
| | | | | | |

Name

Section

Date

**Problem 6-6A Continued**

**Gonzalez Co.**

(a) and (c) (Continued)

Accounts Payable — No. 201

| Date | Explanation | Ref. | Debit | Credit | Balance |
|---|---|---|---|---|---|
| | | | | | |
| | | | | | |
| | | | | | |
| | | | | | |
| | | | | | |
| | | | | | |

L. Gonzalez, Capital — No. 301

| Date | Explanation | Ref. | Debit | Credit | Balance |
|---|---|---|---|---|---|
| | | | | | |
| | | | | | |

Sales — No. 401

| Date | Explanation | Ref. | Debit | Credit | Balance |
|---|---|---|---|---|---|
| | | | | | |
| | | | | | |
| | | | | | |

Sales Returns and Allowances — No. 412

| Date | Explanation | Ref. | Debit | Credit | Balance |
|---|---|---|---|---|---|
| | | | | | |
| | | | | | |

Sales Discounts — No. 414

| Date | Explanation | Ref. | Debit | Credit | Balance |
|---|---|---|---|---|---|
| | | | | | |
| | | | | | |

Cost of Goods Sold — No. 505

| Date | Explanation | Ref. | Debit | Credit | Balance |
|---|---|---|---|---|---|
| | | | | | |
| | | | | | |
| | | | | | |
| | | | | | |
| | | | | | |

Name
Section
Date

**Problem 6-6A Continued**

**Gonzalez Co.**

(a) and (c) (Continued)

Sales Salaries Expense — No. 627

| Date | Explanation | Ref. | Debit | Credit | Balance |
|---|---|---|---|---|---|
| | | | | | |
| | | | | | |

Office Salaries Expense — No. 727

| Date | Explanation | Ref. | Debit | Credit | Balance |
|---|---|---|---|---|---|
| | | | | | |
| | | | | | |

Rent Expense — No. 729

| Date | Explanation | Ref. | Debit | Credit | Balance |
|---|---|---|---|---|---|
| | | | | | |
| | | | | | |

*Accounts Receivable Subsidiary Ledger*

P. Naab

| Date | Explanation | Ref. | Debit | Credit | Balance |
|---|---|---|---|---|---|
| | | | | | |
| | | | | | |
| | | | | | |

K. Hoyt

| Date | Explanation | Ref. | Debit | Credit | Balance |
|---|---|---|---|---|---|
| | | | | | |
| | | | | | |
| | | | | | |

A. Dietz

| Date | Explanation | Ref. | Debit | Credit | Balance |
|---|---|---|---|---|---|
| | | | | | |
| | | | | | |
| | | | | | |

Name **Problem 6-6A Continued**

Section

Date **Gonzalez Co.**

(a) and (c) (Continued)

C. Hernandez

| Date | Explanation | Ref. | Debit | Credit | Balance |
|---|---|---|---|---|---|
| | | | | | |
| | | | | | |
| | | | | | |

*Accounts Payable Subsidiary Ledger*

B. Masoni

| Date | Explanation | Ref. | Debit | Credit | Balance |
|---|---|---|---|---|---|
| | | | | | |
| | | | | | |
| | | | | | |

D. Kraft

| Date | Explanation | Ref. | Debit | Credit | Balance |
|---|---|---|---|---|---|
| | | | | | |
| | | | | | |
| | | | | | |

W. Henrie

| Date | Explanation | Ref. | Debit | Credit | Balance |
|---|---|---|---|---|---|
| | | | | | |
| | | | | | |
| | | | | | |

J. Fanning

| Date | Explanation | Ref. | Debit | Credit | Balance |
|---|---|---|---|---|---|
| | | | | | |
| | | | | | |
| | | | | | |

D. Greer

| Date | Explanation | Ref. | Debit | Credit | Balance |
|---|---|---|---|---|---|
| | | | | | |
| | | | | | |
| | | | | | |

 

Name

Section

Date



(d)

GONZALEZ CO.
Trial Balance
January 31, 1999

| | | Debit | Credit | |
|---|---|---|---|---|
| 1 | Cash | | | 1 |
| 2 | Accounts Receivable | | | 2 |
| 3 | Notes Receivable | | | 3 |
| 4 | Merchandise Inventory | | | 4 |
| 5 | Equipment | | | 5 |
| 6 | Accumulated Depreciation—Equipment | | | 6 |
| 7 | Notes Payable | | | 7 |
| 8 | Accounts Payable | | | 8 |
| 9 | L. Gonzalez, Capital | | | 9 |
| 10 | Sales | | | 10 |
| 11 | Sales Returns and Allowances | | | 11 |
| 12 | Sales Discounts | | | 12 |
| 13 | Cost of Goods Sold | | | 13 |
| 14 | Sales Salaries Expense | | | 14 |
| 15 | Office Salaries Expense | | | 15 |
| 16 | Rent Expense | | | 16 |
| 17 | | | | 17 |
| 18 | | | | 18 |
| 19 | | | | 19 |

(e)

| | | | | |
|---|---|---|---|---|
| 1 | Accounts receivable subsidiary ledger: | | | 1 |
| 2 | | | | 2 |
| 3 | | | | 3 |
| 4 | | | | 4 |
| 5 | | | | 5 |
| 6 | | | | 6 |
| 7 | Accounts receivable control: | | | 7 |
| 8 | | | | 8 |
| 9 | Accounts payable subsidiary ledger: | | | 9 |
| 10 | | | | 10 |
| 11 | | | | 11 |
| 12 | | | | 12 |
| 13 | | | | 13 |
| 14 | | | | 14 |
| 15 | Accounts payable control: | | | 15 |
| 16 | | | | 16 |

Name
Section
Date

**Problem 6-1B**

**Morrow Company**

(a)

MORROW COMPANY
Cash Receipts Journal

CR1

| Date | Account Credited | Ref. | Cash Dr. | Sales Discounts Dr. | Accounts Receivable Cr. | Sales Cr. | Other Accounts Cr. | COGS Dr. Inventory Cr. |
|---|---|---|---|---|---|---|---|---|
| | | | | | | | | |
| | | | | | | | | |
| | | | | | | | | |
| | | | | | | | | |
| | | | | | | | | |
| | | | | | | | | |
| | | | | | | | | |
| | | | | | | | | |
| | | | | | | | | |
| | | | | | | | | |
| | | | | | | | | |
| | | | | | | | | |
| | | | | | | | | |
| | | | | | | | | |
| | | | | | | | | |
| | | | | | | | | |
| | | | | | | | | |
| | | | | | | | | |
| | | | | | | | | |
| | | | | | | | | |
| | | | | | | | | |
| | | | | | | | | |
| | | | | | | | | |
| | | | | | | | | |
| | | | | | | | | |

(b)

*General Ledger*
Accounts Receivable

No.112

| Date | Explanation | Ref. | Debit | Credit | Balance |
|---|---|---|---|---|---|
| | | | | | |
| | | | | | |
| | | | | | |
| | | | | | |

Name
Section
Date

**Problem 6-1B Concluded**

**Morrow Company**

(b) (Continued) *Accounts Receivable Subsidiary Ledger*

Horner

| Date | Explanation | Ref. | Debit | Credit | Balance |
|---|---|---|---|---|---|
| | | | | | |
| | | | | | |
| | | | | | |

Kole

| Date | Explanation | Ref. | Debit | Credit | Balance |
|---|---|---|---|---|---|
| | | | | | |
| | | | | | |

Micci Co.

| Date | Explanation | Ref. | Debit | Credit | Balance |
|---|---|---|---|---|---|
| | | | | | |
| | | | | | |
| | | | | | |

Starr

| Date | Explanation | Ref. | Debit | Credit | Balance |
|---|---|---|---|---|---|
| | | | | | |
| | | | | | |

(c)

Accounts receivable balance:

Sum of subsidiary accounts:

Name

Section

Date

**Problem 6-2B**

**Norton Company**

NORTON COMPANY

(a) Cash Payments Journal CP1

| Date | Ck. No. | Account Debited | Ref. | Other Accounts Dr. | Accounts Payable Dr. | Merchan. Inventory Cr. | Cash Cr. |
|---|---|---|---|---|---|---|---|
| | | | | | | | |
| | | | | | | | |
| | | | | | | | |
| | | | | | | | |
| | | | | | | | |
| | | | | | | | |
| | | | | | | | |
| | | | | | | | |
| | | | | | | | |
| | | | | | | | |
| | | | | | | | |
| | | | | | | | |
| | | | | | | | |
| | | | | | | | |
| | | | | | | | |
| | | | | | | | |
| | | | | | | | |
| | | | | | | | |
| | | | | | | | |
| | | | | | | | |
| | | | | | | | |
| | | | | | | | |
| | | | | | | | |
| | | | | | | | |
| | | | | | | | |

(b)

*General Ledger*

Accounts Payable

No. 201

| Date | Explanation | Ref. | Debit | Credit | Balance |
|---|---|---|---|---|---|
| | | | | | |
| | | | | | |
| | | | | | |
| | | | | | |

Name | **Problem 6-2B Concluded**

Section

Date | **Norton Company**

(b) (Continued)

*Accounts Payable Subsidiary Ledger*

Heston Company

| Date | Explanation | Ref. | Debit | Credit | Balance |
|---|---|---|---|---|---|
| | | | | | |
| | | | | | |
| | | | | | |

Menke & Sons

| Date | Explanation | Ref. | Debit | Credit | Balance |
|---|---|---|---|---|---|
| | | | | | |
| | | | | | |
| | | | | | |

Paige Company

| Date | Explanation | Ref. | Debit | Credit | Balance |
|---|---|---|---|---|---|
| | | | | | |
| | | | | | |
| | | | | | |

Ogle

| Date | Explanation | Ref. | Debit | Credit | Balance |
|---|---|---|---|---|---|
| | | | | | |
| | | | | | |
| | | | | | |

(c)

| | | |
|---|---|---|
| 1 | Accounts payable balance: | 1 |
| 2 | | 2 |
| 3 | | 3 |
| 4 | Sum of subsidiary accounts: | 4 |
| 5 | | 5 |
| 6 | | 6 |
| 7 | | 7 |
| 8 | | 8 |
| 9 | | 9 |
| 10 | | 10 |

Name

Section

Date

**Problem 6-3B**

**Cruz Company**

(a)

CRUZ COMPANY
Purchases Journal

P1

| Date | Account Credited (Debited) | Terms | Ref. | Other Accounts Dr. | Merchan. Inventory Dr. | Accounts Payable Cr. |
|---|---|---|---|---|---|---|
| | | | | | | |

CRUZ COMPANY
Sales Journal

S1

| Date | Account Debited | Invoice No. | Ref. | Accounts Receiv. Dr. Sales Cr. | COGS Dr. Merchandise Inventory Cr. |
|---|---|---|---|---|---|
| | | | | | |

Name

Section

Date

**Problem 6-3B Continued**

**Cruz Company**

(a) (Continued) General Journal G1

| Date | Account Titles and Explanation | Ref. | Debit | Credit |
|---|---|---|---|---|
| | | | | |
| | | | | |
| | | | | |
| | | | | |
| | | | | |
| | | | | |
| | | | | |
| | | | | |
| | | | | |
| | | | | |
| | | | | |
| | | | | |
| | | | | |
| | | | | |
| | | | | |
| | | | | |
| | | | | |
| | | | | |

(b)

*General Ledger*

Accounts Receivable No. 112

| Date | Explanation | Ref. | Debit | Credit | Balance |
|---|---|---|---|---|---|
| | | | | | |
| | | | | | |
| | | | | | |
| | | | | | |

Merchandise Inventory No. 120

| Date | Explanation | Ref. | Debit | Credit | Balance |
|---|---|---|---|---|---|
| | | | | | |
| | | | | | |
| | | | | | |
| | | | | | |
| | | | | | |
| | | | | | |
| | | | | | |
| | | | | | |

Name

Section

Date

**Problem 6-3B Continued**

**Cruz Company**

(b) (Continued)

Supplies — No. 126

| Date | Explanation | Ref. | Debit | Credit | Balance |
|---|---|---|---|---|---|
| | | | | | |
| | | | | | |

Equipment — No. 157

| Date | Explanation | Ref. | Debit | Credit | Balance |
|---|---|---|---|---|---|
| | | | | | |
| | | | | | |

Accounts Payable — No. 201

| Date | Explanation | Ref. | Debit | Credit | Balance |
|---|---|---|---|---|---|
| | | | | | |
| | | | | | |
| | | | | | |
| | | | | | |

Sales — No. 401

| Date | Explanation | Ref. | Debit | Credit | Balance |
|---|---|---|---|---|---|
| | | | | | |
| | | | | | |

Sales Returns and Allowances — No. 412

| Date | Explanation | Ref. | Debit | Credit | Balance |
|---|---|---|---|---|---|
| | | | | | |
| | | | | | |

Cost of Goods Sold — No. 505

| Date | Explanation | Ref. | Debit | Credit | Balance |
|---|---|---|---|---|---|
| | | | | | |
| | | | | | |
| | | | | | |

Advertising Expense — No. 610

| Date | Explanation | Ref. | Debit | Credit | Balance |
|---|---|---|---|---|---|
| | | | | | |
| | | | | | |

Name | **Problem 6-3B Continued**

Section

Date | **Cruz Company**

(b) (Continued)

*Accounts Receivable Subsidiary Ledger*

Flood Bros.

| Date | Explanation | Ref. | Debit | Credit | Balance |
|---|---|---|---|---|---|
| | | | | | |
| | | | | | |
| | | | | | |

Laird Co.

| Date | Explanation | Ref. | Debit | Credit | Balance |
|---|---|---|---|---|---|
| | | | | | |
| | | | | | |
| | | | | | |
| | | | | | |

Marquez Company

| Date | Explanation | Ref. | Debit | Credit | Balance |
|---|---|---|---|---|---|
| | | | | | |
| | | | | | |
| | | | | | |

Resch Company

| Date | Explanation | Ref. | Debit | Credit | Balance |
|---|---|---|---|---|---|
| | | | | | |
| | | | | | |

*Accounts Payable Subsidiary Ledger*

Beyer Supply

| Date | Explanation | Ref. | Debit | Credit | Balance |
|---|---|---|---|---|---|
| | | | | | |
| | | | | | |
| | | | | | |

Carlin Shipping

| Date | Explanation | Ref. | Debit | Credit | Balance |
|---|---|---|---|---|---|
| | | | | | |
| | | | | | |
| | | | | | |

(b) (Continued)

DeVito Company

| Date | Explanation | Ref. | Debit | Credit | Balance |
| --- | --- | --- | --- | --- | --- |
| | | | | | |
| | | | | | |
| | | | | | |

Granger Company

| Date | Explanation | Ref. | Debit | Credit | Balance |
| --- | --- | --- | --- | --- | --- |
| | | | | | |
| | | | | | |
| | | | | | |
| | | | | | |

Meyer's Advertisements

| Date | Explanation | Ref. | Debit | Credit | Balance |
| --- | --- | --- | --- | --- | --- |
| | | | | | |
| | | | | | |

Reeble Company

| Date | Explanation | Ref. | Debit | Credit | Balance |
| --- | --- | --- | --- | --- | --- |
| | | | | | |
| | | | | | |

Name

Section

Date

**Problem 6-3B Concluded**

**Cruz Company**

(c)

Accounts receivable balance:

Sum of subsidiary accounts:

Accounts payable balance:

Sum of subsidiary accounts:

Name

Section

Date

**Problem 6-4E**

**Shell Company**

(a), (b), and (c)

SHELL COMPANY
Sales Journal

S1

| Date | Account Debited | Invoice No. | Ref. | Accounts Receiv. Dr. Sales Cr. | COGS Dr. Merchandise Inventory Cr. |
|---|---|---|---|---|---|
| | | | | | |
| | | | | | |
| | | | | | |
| | | | | | |
| | | | | | |
| | | | | | |
| | | | | | |
| | | | | | |
| | | | | | |

SHELL COMPANY
Purchases Journal

P1

| Date | Account Credited | Terms | Ref. | Merchandise Inventory (Dr.) Acc. Pay. (Cr.) |
|---|---|---|---|---|
| | | | | |
| | | | | |
| | | | | |
| | | | | |
| | | | | |
| | | | | |
| | | | | |
| | | | | |
| | | | | |
| | | | | |

General Journal

G1

| | | | | | |
|---|---|---|---|---|---|
| 1 | | | | | 1 |
| 2 | | | | | 2 |
| 3 | | | | | 3 |
| 4 | | | | | 4 |
| 5 | | | | | 5 |
| 6 | | | | | 6 |
| 7 | | | | | 7 |
| 8 | | | | | 8 |
| 9 | | | | | 9 |

Name

Section

Date

**Problem 6-4B Concluded**

**Shell Company**

(a), (b), and (c) (Continued)

SHELL COMPANY

Cash Receipts Journal

CR1

| Date | Account Credited | Ref. | Cash Dr. | Sales Discounts Dr. | Accounts Receivable Cr. | Sales Cr. | Other Accounts Cr. | COGS Dr. Inventory Cr. |
|---|---|---|---|---|---|---|---|---|
| | | | | | | | | |
| | | | | | | | | |
| | | | | | | | | |
| | | | | | | | | |
| | | | | | | | | |
| | | | | | | | | |
| | | | | | | | | |
| | | | | | | | | |
| | | | | | | | | |
| | | | | | | | | |
| | | | | | | | | |
| | | | | | | | | |
| | | | | | | | | |
| | | | | | | | | |

SHELL COMPANY

Cash Payments Journal

CP1

| Date | Account Debited | Ref. | Other Accounts Dr. | Accounts Payable Dr. | Merchan. Inventory Cr. | Cash Cr. |
|---|---|---|---|---|---|---|
| | | | | | | |
| | | | | | | |
| | | | | | | |
| | | | | | | |
| | | | | | | |
| | | | | | | |
| | | | | | | |
| | | | | | | |
| | | | | | | |
| | | | | | | |
| | | | | | | |
| | | | | | | |

Name

Section

Date

**Problem 6-5B**

**Weber Co.**

(a), (d) and (g)

*General Ledger*

Cash — No. 101

| Date | Explanation | Ref. | Debit | Credit | Balance |
|---|---|---|---|---|---|
| | | | | | |
| | | | | | |
| | | | | | |

Accounts Receivable — No. 112

| Date | Explanation | Ref. | Debit | Credit | Balance |
|---|---|---|---|---|---|
| | | | | | |
| | | | | | |
| | | | | | |

Merchandise Inventory — No. 120

| Date | Explanation | Ref. | Debit | Credit | Balance |
|---|---|---|---|---|---|
| | | | | | |
| | | | | | |
| | | | | | |
| | | | | | |
| | | | | | |
| | | | | | |

Store Supplies — No. 127

| Date | Explanation | Ref. | Debit | Credit | Balance |
|---|---|---|---|---|---|
| | | | | | |
| | | | | | |
| | | | | | |

Prepaid Rent — No. 131

| Date | Explanation | Ref. | Debit | Credit | Balance |
|---|---|---|---|---|---|
| | | | | | |
| | | | | | |
| | | | | | |

Accounts Payable — No. 201

| Date | Explanation | Ref. | Debit | Credit | Balance |
|---|---|---|---|---|---|
| | | | | | |
| | | | | | |
| | | | | | |

Name　　　　**Problem 6-5B Continued**

Section

Date　　　　**Weber Co.**

(a), (d) and (g) (Continued)

Weber, Capital　　No. 301

| Date | Explanation | Ref. | Debit | Credit | Balance |
|---|---|---|---|---|---|
| | | | | | |
| | | | | | |

Weber, Drawing　　No. 306

| Date | Explanation | Ref. | Debit | Credit | Balance |
|---|---|---|---|---|---|
| | | | | | |
| | | | | | |

Sales　　No. 401

| Date | Explanation | Ref. | Debit | Credit | Balance |
|---|---|---|---|---|---|
| | | | | | |
| | | | | | |
| | | | | | |

Sales Returns and Allowances　　No. 412

| Date | Explanation | Ref. | Debit | Credit | Balance |
|---|---|---|---|---|---|
| | | | | | |
| | | | | | |

Sales Discounts　　No. 414

| Date | Explanation | Ref. | Debit | Credit | Balance |
|---|---|---|---|---|---|
| | | | | | |
| | | | | | |

Cost of Goods Sold　　No. 505

| Date | Explanation | Ref. | Debit | Credit | Balance |
|---|---|---|---|---|---|
| | | | | | |
| | | | | | |
| | | | | | |
| | | | | | |

Supplies Expense　　No. 631

| Date | Explanation | Ref. | Debit | Credit | Balance |
|---|---|---|---|---|---|
| | | | | | |
| | | | | | |

(a), (d) and (g) (Continued)

Rent Expense | No. 729

| Date | Explanation | Ref. | Debit | Credit | Balance |
|---|---|---|---|---|---|
| | | | | | |
| | | | | | |

(b)

WEBER CO.
Cash Receipts Journal | CR1

| Date | Account Credited | Ref. | Cash Dr. | Sales Discounts Dr. | Accounts Receivable Cr. | Sales Cr. | Other Accounts Cr. | COGS Dr. Inventory Cr. |
|---|---|---|---|---|---|---|---|---|
| | | | | | | | | |
| | | | | | | | | |
| | | | | | | | | |
| | | | | | | | | |
| | | | | | | | | |
| | | | | | | | | |
| | | | | | | | | |
| | | | | | | | | |
| | | | | | | | | |
| | | | | | | | | |
| | | | | | | | | |
| | | | | | | | | |
| | | | | | | | | |
| | | | | | | | | |

WEBER CO.
Sales Journal | S1

| Date | Account Debited | Invoice No. | Ref. | Accounts Receiv. Dr. Sales Cr. | COGS Dr. Merchandise Inventory Cr. |
|---|---|---|---|---|---|
| | | | | | |
| | | | | | |
| | | | | | |
| | | | | | |
| | | | | | |
| | | | | | |
| | | | | | |
| | | | | | |
| | | | | | |
| | | | | | |

Name | Problem 6-5B Continued

Section

Date | **Weber Co.**

(c) *Accounts Payable Subsidiary Ledger*

C. Hunt

| Date | Explanation | Ref. | Debit | Credit | Balance |
|---|---|---|---|---|---|
| | | | | | |
| | | | | | |
| | | | | | |
| | | | | | |

S. Faur

| Date | Explanation | Ref. | Debit | Credit | Balance |
|---|---|---|---|---|---|
| | | | | | |
| | | | | | |
| | | | | | |
| | | | | | |

R. Jenks

| Date | Explanation | Ref. | Debit | Credit | Balance |
|---|---|---|---|---|---|
| | | | | | |
| | | | | | |
| | | | | | |

P. Coley

| Date | Explanation | Ref. | Debit | Credit | Balance |
|---|---|---|---|---|---|
| | | | | | |
| | | | | | |
| | | | | | |
| | | | | | |

B. Goltra

| Date | Explanation | Ref. | Debit | Credit | Balance |
|---|---|---|---|---|---|
| | | | | | |
| | | | | | |
| | | | | | |

Name

Section

Date

**Problem 6-5B Continued**

**Weber Co.**

(c) (Continued)

*Accounts Receivable Subsidiary Ledger*

Lentz Co.

| Date | Explanation | Ref. | Debit | Credit | Balance |
|---|---|---|---|---|---|
| | | | | | |
| | | | | | |
| | | | | | |
| | | | | | |

A. Kear

| Date | Explanation | Ref. | Debit | Credit | Balance |
|---|---|---|---|---|---|
| | | | | | |
| | | | | | |
| | | | | | |

G. Linton

| Date | Explanation | Ref. | Debit | Credit | Balance |
|---|---|---|---|---|---|
| | | | | | |
| | | | | | |
| | | | | | |
| | | | | | |

J. Wegner

| Date | Explanation | Ref. | Debit | Credit | Balance |
|---|---|---|---|---|---|
| | | | | | |
| | | | | | |
| | | | | | |
| | | | | | |

(e)

WEBER CO.
Trial Balance
July 31, 1999

| | | Debit | Credit | |
|---|---|---|---|---|
| 1 | Cash | | | 1 |
| 2 | Accounts Receivable | | | 2 |
| 3 | Merchandise Inventory | | | 3 |
| 4 | Store Supplies | | | 4 |
| 5 | Prepaid Rent | | | 5 |
| 6 | Accounts Payable | | | 6 |
| 7 | Weber, Capital | | | 7 |
| 8 | Weber, Drawing | | | 8 |
| 9 | Sales | | | 9 |
| 10 | Sales Discounts | | | 10 |
| 11 | Cost of Goods Sold | | | 11 |
| 12 | | | | 12 |
| 13 | | | | 13 |
| 14 | | | | 14 |
| 15 | | | | 15 |

(f)

| | | | | |
|---|---|---|---|---|
| 1 | | | | 1 |
| 2 | Accounts receivable control account: | | | 2 |
| 3 | | | | 3 |
| 4 | Accounts receivable subsidiary accounts: | | | 4 |
| 5 | | | | 5 |
| 6 | | | | 6 |
| 7 | | | | 7 |
| 8 | | | | 8 |
| 9 | Accounts payable control account: | | | 9 |
| 10 | | | | 10 |
| 11 | Accounts payable subsidiary accounts: | | | 11 |
| 12 | | | | 12 |
| 13 | | | | 13 |
| 14 | | | | 14 |
| 15 | | | | 15 |

| Name | Problem 6-5B Concluded |
|---|---|
| Section | |
| Date | Weber Co. |

(b) and (g)

**General Journal** G1

| Date | Account Titles and Explanation | Ref. | Debit | Credit |
|---|---|---|---|---|
| | | | | |
| | | | | |
| | | | | |
| | | | | |
| | | | | |
| | | | | |
| | | | | |
| | | | | |
| | | | | |
| | | | | |
| | | | | |
| | | | | |
| | | | | |
| | | | | |
| | | | | |

(h)

**WEBER CO.**
**Adjusted Trial Balance**
**July 31, 1999**

| | Debit | Credit |
|---|---|---|
| Cash | | |
| Accounts Receivable | | |
| Merchandise Inventory | | |
| Store Supplies | | |
| Prepaid Rent | | |
| Accounts Payable | | |
| Weber, Capital | | |
| Weber, Drawing | | |
| Sales | | |
| Sales Discounts | | |
| Cost of Goods Sold | | |
| Supplies Expense | | |
| Rent Expense | | |
| | | |
| | | |

(a)

STONE CO.
Sales Journal S1

| Date | Account Debited | Invoice No. | Ref. | Accounts Receiv. Dr. Sales Cr. | COGS Dr. Merchan. Inventory Cr. |
|---|---|---|---|---|---|
| | | | | | |
| | | | | | |
| | | | | | |
| | | | | | |
| | | | | | |
| | | | | | |
| | | | | | |
| | | | | | |
| | | | | | |
| | | | | | |
| | | | | | |
| | | | | | |
| | | | | | |
| | | | | | |
| | | | | | |
| | | | | | |

STONE CO.
Purchases Journal P1

| Date | Account Credited | Terms | Ref. | Merchandise Inventory Dr. Acc. Pay. Cr. |
|---|---|---|---|---|
| | | | | |
| | | | | |
| | | | | |
| | | | | |
| | | | | |
| | | | | |
| | | | | |
| | | | | |
| | | | | |
| | | | | |
| | | | | |
| | | | | |
| | | | | |
| | | | | |
| | | | | |
| | | | | |

 

(a) (Continued)

STONE CO.
Cash Receipts Journal

CR1

| Date | Account Credited | Ref. | Cash Dr. | Sales Discounts Dr. | Accounts Receivable Cr. | Sales Cr. | Other Accounts Cr. | COGS Dr. Inventory Cr. |
|---|---|---|---|---|---|---|---|---|
| | | | | | | | | |

Name

Section

Date



(a) (Continued)

STONE CO.

Cash Payments Journal

CR1

| Date | Account Debited | Ref. | Other Accounts Dr. | Accounts Payable Dr. | Office Supplies Dr. | Merchan. Inventory Cr. | Cash Cr. |
|---|---|---|---|---|---|---|---|
| | | | | | | | |
| | | | | | | | |
| | | | | | | | |
| | | | | | | | |
| | | | | | | | |
| | | | | | | | |
| | | | | | | | |
| | | | | | | | |
| | | | | | | | |
| | | | | | | | |
| | | | | | | | |
| | | | | | | | |
| | | | | | | | |
| | | | | | | | |
| | | | | | | | |
| | | | | | | | |
| | | | | | | | |
| | | | | | | | |
| | | | | | | | |
| | | | | | | | |
| | | | | | | | |
| | | | | | | | |
| | | | | | | | |
| | | | | | | | |
| | | | | | | | |
| | | | | | | | |
| | | | | | | | |
| | | | | | | | |
| | | | | | | | |
| | | | | | | | |

Name

Section

Date



(a) (Continued) General Journal G1

| Date | Account Titles and Explanation | Ref. | Debit | Credit |
|---|---|---|---|---|

 

(b) and (e)

*General Ledger*

Cash — No. 101

| Date | Explanation | Ref. | Debit | Credit | Balance |
|---|---|---|---|---|---|
| Jan. 1 | Balance | ✓ | | | 35750 |
| | | | | | |
| | | | | | |
| | | | | | |

Accounts Receivable — No. 112

| Date | Explanation | Ref. | Debit | Credit | Balance |
|---|---|---|---|---|---|
| Jan. 1 | Balance | ✓ | | | 13000 |
| | | | | | |
| | | | | | |
| | | | | | |
| | | | | | |

Notes Receivable — No. 115

| Date | Explanation | Ref. | Debit | Credit | Balance |
|---|---|---|---|---|---|
| Jan. 1 | Balance | ✓ | | | 39000 |
| | | | | | |
| | | | | | |

Merchandise Inventory — No. 120

| Date | Explanation | Ref. | Debit | Credit | Balance |
|---|---|---|---|---|---|
| Jan. 1 | Balance | ✓ | | | 18000 |
| | | | | | |
| | | | | | |
| | | | | | |
| | | | | | |
| | | | | | |
| | | | | | |
| | | | | | |

Office Supplies — No. 125

| Date | Explanation | Ref. | Debit | Credit | Balance |
|---|---|---|---|---|---|
| Jan. 1 | Balance | ✓ | | | 1000 |
| | | | | | |
| | | | | | |
| | | | | | |

(b) and (e) (Continued)

Prepaid Insurance — No. 130

| Date | Explanation | Ref. | Debit | Credit | Balance |
|---|---|---|---|---|---|
| Jan. 1 | Balance | ✓ | | | 2000 |
| | | | | | |
| | | | | | |

Equipment — No. 157

| Date | Explanation | Ref. | Debit | Credit | Balance |
|---|---|---|---|---|---|
| Jan. 1 | Balance | ✓ | | | 6450 |
| | | | | | |
| | | | | | |

Accumulated Depreciation — Equipment — No. 158

| Date | Explanation | Ref. | Debit | Credit | Balance |
|---|---|---|---|---|---|
| Jan. 1 | Balance | ✓ | | | 1500 |
| | | | | | |
| | | | | | |

Notes Payable — No. 200

| Date | Explanation | Ref. | Debit | Credit | Balance |
|---|---|---|---|---|---|
| | | | | | |
| | | | | | |
| | | | | | |

Accounts Payable — No. 201

| Date | Explanation | Ref. | Debit | Credit | Balance |
|---|---|---|---|---|---|
| Jan. 1 | Balance | ✓ | | | 35000 |
| | | | | | |
| | | | | | |
| | | | | | |
| | | | | | |
| | | | | | |

Interest Payable — No. 230

| Date | Explanation | Ref. | Debit | Credit | Balance |
|---|---|---|---|---|---|
| | | | | | |
| | | | | | |
| | | | | | |

(b) and (e) (Continued)

M. Stone, Capital No. 301

| Date | Explanation | Ref. | Debit | Credit | Balance |
|---|---|---|---|---|---|
| Jan. 1 | Balance | ✓ | | | 78700 |
| | | | | | |
| | | | | | |
| | | | | | |

M. Stone, Drawing No. 306

| Date | Explanation | Ref. | Debit | Credit | Balance |
|---|---|---|---|---|---|
| | | | | | |
| | | | | | |
| | | | | | |

Income Summary No. 350

| Date | Explanation | Ref. | Debit | Credit | Balance |
|---|---|---|---|---|---|
| | | | | | |
| | | | | | |
| | | | | | |
| | | | | | |

Sales No. 401

| Date | Explanation | Ref. | Debit | Credit | Balance |
|---|---|---|---|---|---|
| | | | | | |
| | | | | | |
| | | | | | |
| | | | | | |

Sales Returns and Allowances No. 412

| Date | Explanation | Ref. | Debit | Credit | Balance |
|---|---|---|---|---|---|
| | | | | | |
| | | | | | |
| | | | | | |

(b) and (e) (Continued)

Sales Discounts No. 414

| Date | Explanation | Ref. | Debit | Credit | Balance |
|---|---|---|---|---|---|
| | | | | | |
| | | | | | |
| | | | | | |
| | | | | | |

Interest Revenue No. 430

| Date | Explanation | Ref. | Debit | Credit | Balance |
|---|---|---|---|---|---|
| | | | | | |
| | | | | | |
| | | | | | |

Cost of Goods Sold No. 505

| Date | Explanation | Ref. | Debit | Credit | Balance |
|---|---|---|---|---|---|
| | | | | | |
| | | | | | |
| | | | | | |
| | | | | | |

Sales Salaries Expense No. 627

| Date | Explanation | Ref. | Debit | Credit | Balance |
|---|---|---|---|---|---|
| | | | | | |
| | | | | | |
| | | | | | |

 

(b) and (e) (Continued)

Depreciation Expense — No. 711

| Date | Explanation | Ref. | Debit | Credit | Balance |
|---|---|---|---|---|---|
| | | | | | |
| | | | | | |
| | | | | | |

Interest Expense — No. 718

| Date | Explanation | Ref. | Debit | Credit | Balance |
|---|---|---|---|---|---|
| | | | | | |
| | | | | | |
| | | | | | |

Insurance Expense — No. 722

| Date | Explanation | Ref. | Debit | Credit | Balance |
|---|---|---|---|---|---|
| | | | | | |
| | | | | | |
| | | | | | |

Office Salaries Expense — No. 727

| Date | Explanation | Ref. | Debit | Credit | Balance |
|---|---|---|---|---|---|
| | | | | | |
| | | | | | |
| | | | | | |

Office Supplies Expense — No. 728

| Date | Explanation | Ref. | Debit | Credit | Balance |
|---|---|---|---|---|---|
| | | | | | |
| | | | | | |
| | | | | | |

Rent Expense — No. 729

| Date | Explanation | Ref. | Debit | Credit | Balance |
|---|---|---|---|---|---|
| | | | | | |
| | | | | | |
| | | | | | |

(b) and (e) (Continued)

*Accounts Receivable Subsidiary Ledger*

R. Dansig

| Date | Explanation | Ref. | Debit | Credit | Balance |
|---|---|---|---|---|---|
| Jan. 1 | Balance | ✓ | | | 1500 |
| | | | | | |
| | | | | | |
| | | | | | |

J. Eaton

| Date | Explanation | Ref. | Debit | Credit | Balance |
|---|---|---|---|---|---|
| | | | | | |
| | | | | | |
| | | | | | |
| | | | | | |
| | | | | | |

B. Jaggar

| Date | Explanation | Ref. | Debit | Credit | Balance |
|---|---|---|---|---|---|
| Jan. 1 | Balance | ✓ | | | 7500 |
| | | | | | |
| | | | | | |
| | | | | | |

S. Lowell

| Date | Explanation | Ref. | Debit | Credit | Balance |
|---|---|---|---|---|---|
| Jan. 1 | Balance | ✓ | | | 4000 |
| | | | | | |
| | | | | | |
| | | | | | |
| | | | | | |

B. Sargent

| Date | Explanation | Ref. | Debit | Credit | Balance |
|---|---|---|---|---|---|
| | | | | | |
| | | | | | |
| | | | | | |
| | | | | | |

(b) and (e) (Continued)

*Accounts Payable Subsidiary Ledger*

D. Landell

| Date | Explanation | Ref. | Debit | Credit | Balance |
|---|---|---|---|---|---|
| | | | | | |
| | | | | | |
| | | | | | |

S. Lee

| Date | Explanation | Ref. | Debit | Credit | Balance |
|---|---|---|---|---|---|
| Jan. 1 | Balance | ✓ | | | 9000 |
| | | | | | |
| | | | | | |
| | | | | | |
| | | | | | |
| | | | | | |

R. Mannon

| Date | Explanation | Ref. | Debit | Credit | Balance |
|---|---|---|---|---|---|
| Jan. 1 | Balance | ✓ | | | 15000 |
| | | | | | |
| | | | | | |

D. Nordin

| Date | Explanation | Ref. | Debit | Credit | Balance |
|---|---|---|---|---|---|
| Jan. 1 | Balance | ✓ | | | 11000 |
| | | | | | |
| | | | | | |
| | | | | | |
| | | | | | |
| | | | | | |

S. Walden

| Date | Explanation | Ref. | Debit | Credit | Balance |
|---|---|---|---|---|---|
| | | | | | |
| | | | | | |
| | | | | | |
| | | | | | |

Name

Section

Date



Additional working papers for this practice set are at the back of this book

(d)

STONE CO.

Income Statement

For the Month Ended January 31, 1999

Name

Section

Date





(d) (Continued)

STONE CO.
Owner's Equity Statement
For the Month Ended January 31, 1999

STONE CO.
Balance Sheet
January 31, 1999

Assets

Liabilities and Owner's Equity

Name

Section

Date



(e)

General Journal

G1

| Date | Account Titles and Explanation | Ref. | Debit | Credit |
| --- | --- | --- | --- | --- |
| | Closing Entries | | | |

Name

Section

Date

Stone Co. (Mini Practice Set)

(f)

STONE CO.
Post-Closing Trial Balance
January 31, 1999

| | Debit | Credit |
|---|---|---|
| Cash | | |
| Notes Receivable | | |
| Accounts Receivable | | |
| Merchandise Inventory | | |
| Office Supplies | | |
| Prepaid Insurance | | |
| Equipment | | |
| Accumulated Depreciation—Equipment | | |
| Notes Payable | | |
| Accounts Payable | | |
| Interest Payable | | |
| M. Stone, Capital | | |
| | | |
| | | |
| | | |

| | | |
|---|---|---|
| | | |
| Accounts receivable balance: | | |
| | | |
| | | |
| Sum of subsidiary accounts: | | |
| | | |
| | | |
| | | |
| | | |
| | | |
| | | |
| Accounts payable balance: | | |
| | | |
| | | |
| Sum of subsidiary accounts: | | |
| | | |
| | | |
| | | |
| | | |
| | | |

Name

Section

Date



(a)

Name

Section

Date



(a) (Continued)

(b)

(c)

Name

Section

Date



**REAL-WORLD FOCUS** Alco Standard Corporation

(a)

(b)

**ETHICS CASE** Tyler Products Company

Name

Section

Date

Name

Section

Date

Name

Section

Date

Name

Section

Date

**Exercise 7-1**

**Galenti's Pizza**

1.

2.

3.

4.

5.

6.

Name

Section

Date

**Exercise 7-2**

**Seymor Company**

| (a) | | (b) |
|---|---|---|
| Weakness | Principle Violated | Recommended Change |
| 1. | | |
| 2. | | |
| 3. | | |
| 4. | | |
| 5. | | |

Name

Section

Date

**Exercise 7-3**

**Hilga's Boutique Shoppe**

| (a) | | (b) |
|---|---|---|
| Weakness | Principle Violated | Suggested Improvement |
| 1. | | |
| 2. | | |
| 3. | | |
| 4. | | |
| 5. | | |

Name

Section

Date

**Vermont Company**

| (a) Weaknesses | (b) Suggested Improvement |
|---|---|
| 1. | |
| | |
| | |
| 2. | |
| | |
| | |
| 3. | |
| | |
| | |
| 4. | |
| | |
| | |
| 5. | |
| | |
| | |
| 6. | |
| | |
| | |
| 7. | |
| | |
| | |
| 8. | |
| | |
| | |
| | |

Name

Section

Date



**#5**

**#6**

(a)

ALANA DAVIS COMPANY

Bank Reconciliation

January 31

(b)

Name
Section
Date



**#7**

**#8** (a)

CODY CAMERA COMPANY
Bank Reconciliation
July 31

(b)

Name

**Exercise 7-9**

Section

Date

**Mawmeg Company**

(a)

MAWMEG COMPANY

Bank Reconciliation

September 30

(b)

Name **Exercise 7-10**

Section

Date **Chi Chi Company**

(a)

(b)

(c)

(d)

Section

Date



(a)

| Principles | Application to Burlington Theater |
| --- | --- |

(b)

Name **Problem 7-2A**

Section

Date **ABM Company**

General Journal

| Date | Account Titles and Explanation | Ref. | Debit | Credit |
|---|---|---|---|---|

(b)

Petty Cash

| Date | Explanation | Ref. | Debit | Credit | Balance |
|---|---|---|---|---|---|
| | | | | | |
| | | | | | |
| | | | | | |
| | | | | | |

(c)

| | |
|---|---|
| 1 | 1 |
| 2 | 2 |
| 3 | 3 |
| 4 | 4 |
| 5 | 5 |
| 6 | 6 |
| 7 | 7 |
| 8 | 8 |
| 9 | 9 |
| 10 | 10 |
| 11 | 11 |
| 12 | 12 |
| 13 | 13 |
| 14 | 14 |
| 15 | 15 |

Name **Problem 7-3A**

Section

Date **Long Company**

(a)

LONG COMPANY

Bank Reconciliation

July 31, 1999

(b) General Journal

| Date | Account Titles and Explanation | Ref. | Debit | Credit |
|---|---|---|---|---|

Name

Section

Date

**Problem 7-4A**

**Zurich Company**

(a)

ZURICH COMPANY

Bank Reconciliation

November 30, 1999

(b) General Journal

| Date | Account Titles and Explanation | Ref. | Debit | Credit |
|---|---|---|---|---|

Name  **Problem 7-5A**

Section

Date  **Melo Company**

(a)

MELO COMPANY

Bank Reconciliation

August 31, 1999

Computations

Name **Problem 7-5A Concluded**

Section

Date **Melo Company**

(b)

General Journal

| | Date | Account Titles and Explanation | Ref. | Debit | Credit | |
|---|---|---|---|---|---|---|
| 1 | | | | | | 1 |
| 2 | | | | | | 2 |
| 3 | | | | | | 3 |
| 4 | | | | | | 4 |
| 5 | | | | | | 5 |
| 6 | | | | | | 6 |
| 7 | | | | | | 7 |
| 8 | | | | | | 8 |
| 9 | | | | | | 9 |
| 10 | | | | | | 10 |
| 11 | | | | | | 11 |
| 12 | | | | | | 12 |
| 13 | | | | | | 13 |
| 14 | | | | | | 14 |
| 15 | | | | | | 15 |
| 16 | | | | | | 16 |
| 17 | | | | | | 17 |
| 18 | | | | | | 18 |
| 19 | | | | | | 19 |
| 20 | | | | | | 20 |

Name **Problem 7-6A**

Section

Date **Giant Company**

(a)

GIANT COMPANY

Bank Reconciliation

October 31, 1999

(b) and (c)

Name
Section
Date

**Problem 7-1B**

**Talley Office Supply Company**

| Principles | Application to Cash Disbursements |
|---|---|

Name

Section

Date

**Problem 7-2B**

**Vickers Company**

General Journal

| Date | Account Titles and Explanation | Ref. | Debit | Credit |
|---|---|---|---|---|

(b)

Petty Cash

| Date | Explanation | Ref. | Debit | Credit | Balance |
| --- | --- | --- | --- | --- | --- |
| | | | | | |
| | | | | | |
| | | | | | |
| | | | | | |

(c)

| |
| --- |
| 1 |
| 2 |
| 3 |
| 4 |
| 5 |
| 6 |
| 7 |
| 8 |
| 9 |
| 10 |
| 11 |
| 12 |
| 13 |
| 14 |
| 15 |

 

Name **Problem 7-3A**

Section

Date **Maris Company**

(a)

MARIS COMPANY
Bank Reconciliation
May 31, 1999

(b)

General Journal

| Date | Account Titles and Explanation | Ref. | Debit | Credit |
|---|---|---|---|---|

Name

Section

Date

**Problem 7-4B**

**Kona Company**

(a)

KONA COMPANY

Bank Reconciliation

December 31, 1999

| | | |
|---|---|---|
| | | |
| | | |
| | | |
| | | |
| | | |
| | | |
| | | |
| | | |
| | | |
| | | |
| | | |
| | | |
| | | |
| | | |
| | | |
| | | |
| | | |
| | | |
| | | |
| | | |
| | | |

(b)

General Journal

| Date | Account Titles and Explanation | Ref. | Debit | Credit |
|---|---|---|---|---|
| | | | | |
| | | | | |
| | | | | |
| | | | | |
| | | | | |
| | | | | |
| | | | | |
| | | | | |
| | | | | |
| | | | | |
| | | | | |
| | | | | |
| | | | | |
| | | | | |

Name _______________ **Problem 7-5B**

Section _______________

Date _______________ **Aluminum Company**

(a)

ALUMINUM COMPANY

Bank Reconciliation

July 31, 1999

Computations

Name

Section

Date

**Problem 7-5B Concluded**

**Aluminum Company**

(b) General Journal

| Date | Account Titles and Explanation | Ref. | Debit | Credit |
|---|---|---|---|---|
| | | | | |
| | | | | |
| | | | | |
| | | | | |
| | | | | |
| | | | | |
| | | | | |
| | | | | |
| | | | | |
| | | | | |
| | | | | |
| | | | | |
| | | | | |
| | | | | |
| | | | | |
| | | | | |
| | | | | |
| | | | | |
| | | | | |
| | | | | |

Name

Section

Date



(a)

(b)

(c)

(d)

Name
Section
Date

| (a) (In millions) | Kellogg | General Mills |
| --- | --- | --- |
| 1. Cash and cash equivalents at year-end 1997 | | |
| 2. Increase/decrease in cash and cash equivalents from 1996 to 1997 | | |
| 3. Cash provided by operating activities during fiscal year 1997 | | |

(b)

Name

Section

Date

Microsoft, Inc. and Oracle

(a)

(b)

(c)

(d)

(e)

Name

Section

Date



(a)

(b)

(c)

Name ______________________ **Chapter 7 Real-World Focus**

Section ______________________

Date ______________________ **Chapter 7 Ethics Case**

**REAL-WORLD FOCUS** Alternative Distributor Corp.

| Material Weakness | Internal Control Principle |
| --- | --- |
| | |

**ETHICS CASE** Bad Water Bottling Company

(a)

(b)

(c)

Name

Section

Date

Name

Section

Date

Name

Section

Date

Name

Section

Date

**Exercises 8-1 to 8-2**

**#1**

**#2**

 

Name

Section

Date

#3 (a)

(b)

#4

Name

Section

Date

**Exercises 8-5 to 8-**

**#5**

**#6**

Name

Section

Date



**#7** (a)

(b)

**#8**

Name

Section

Date

**Exercises 8-9 to 8-1**

**#9**

**#10**

Name

Section

Date

**Problem 8-1A**

**Mike Muzillo Imports**

(a)

General Journal

| | Date | Account Titles and Explanation | Ref. | Debit | Credit | |
|---|---|---|---|---|---|---|
| 1 | | | | | | 1 |
| 2 | | | | | | 2 |
| 3 | | | | | | 3 |
| 4 | | | | | | 4 |
| 5 | | | | | | 5 |
| 6 | | | | | | 6 |
| 7 | | | | | | 7 |
| 8 | | | | | | 8 |
| 9 | | | | | | 9 |
| 10 | | | | | | 10 |
| 11 | | | | | | 11 |
| 12 | | | | | | 12 |
| 13 | | | | | | 13 |
| 14 | | | | | | 14 |
| 15 | | | | | | 15 |
| 16 | | | | | | 16 |
| 17 | | | | | | 17 |
| 18 | | | | | | 18 |
| 19 | | | | | | 19 |
| 20 | | | | | | 20 |

(b)

ACCOUNTS RECEIVABLE

ALLOWANCE FOR DOUBTFUL ACCOUNTS

(c)

(d)

Name

Section

Date

**Problem 8-2A**

**Tisinai Company**

(a)

(b)

(c)

(d)

(e)

Name

Section

Date

**Problem 8-3A**

**Chris Cain Company**

(a), (b), and (c)

General Journal

| Date | Account Titles and Explanation | Ref. | Debit | Credit |
|---|---|---|---|---|
| (a) | | | | |
| | | | | |
| | | | | |
| | | | | |
| | | | | |
| (b) | | | | |
| | | | | |
| | | | | |
| | | | | |
| | | | | |
| | | | | |
| | | | | |
| | | | | |
| | | | | |
| | | | | |
| | | | | |
| | | | | |
| | | | | |
| (c) | | | | |
| | | | | |
| | | | | |
| | | | | |

(a) and (b)

Bad Debts Expense

| Date | Explanation | Ref. | Debit | Credit | Balance |
|---|---|---|---|---|---|
| | | | | | |
| | | | | | |
| | | | | | |

Allowance for Doubtful Accounts

| Date | Explanation | Ref. | Debit | Credit | Balance |
|---|---|---|---|---|---|
| | | | | | |
| | | | | | |
| | | | | | |
| | | | | | |
| | | | | | |
| | | | | | |
| | | | | | |

Name  **Problem 8-4A**

Section

Date  **John Gleason Company**

General Journal

| Date | Account Titles and Explanation | Ref. | Debit | Credit |
|---|---|---|---|---|
| (a) | | | | |
| (b) | | | | |
| (c) | | | | |
| (d) | | | | |
| (e) | | | | |

(f)

Name

Section

Date

**Problem 8-5**

**Connie Kolzow Co**

(a) General Journal

| Date | Account Titles and Explanation | Ref. | Debit | Credit |
|---|---|---|---|---|

 

Name
Section
Date

**Problem 8-5A Concluded**

**Connie Kolzow Co.**

(b)

Notes Receivable

| Date | Explanation | Ref. | Debit | Credit | Balance |
|---|---|---|---|---|---|
| | | | | | |
| | | | | | |
| | | | | | |
| | | | | | |
| | | | | | |

Accounts Receivable

| Date | Explanation | Ref. | Debit | Credit | Balance |
|---|---|---|---|---|---|
| | | | | | |
| | | | | | |
| | | | | | |
| | | | | | |
| | | | | | |

Interest Receivable

| Date | Explanation | Ref. | Debit | Credit | Balance |
|---|---|---|---|---|---|
| | | | | | |
| | | | | | |
| | | | | | |
| | | | | | |
| | | | | | |
| | | | | | |

(c)

CONNIE KOLZOW CO.
Balance Sheet (Partial)
December 31, 1999

| | | |
|---|---|---|
| Assets | | |
| Current Assets | | |
| | | |
| | | |
| | | |
| | | |
| | | |
| | | |

Name

Section

Date

**Problem 8-6A**

**Judy Elam Company**

General Journal

| Date | Account Titles and Explanation | Ref. | Debit | Credit |
|---|---|---|---|---|

Name — **Problem 8-1B**

Section

Date — **Cellular Ten Inc.**

(a) General Journal

| Date | Account Titles and Explanation | Ref. | Debit | Credit |
| --- | --- | --- | --- | --- |
| | | | | |
| | | | | |
| | | | | |
| | | | | |
| | | | | |
| | | | | |
| | | | | |
| | | | | |
| | | | | |
| | | | | |
| | | | | |
| | | | | |
| | | | | |
| | | | | |
| | | | | |
| | | | | |
| | | | | |
| | | | | |
| | | | | |
| | | | | |

(b)

| ACCOUNTS RECEIVABLE | | ALLOWANCE FOR DOUBTFUL ACCOUNTS | |
| --- | --- | --- | --- |
| | | | |

(c)

(d)

Name **Problem 8-2B**

Section

Date **Sue Hohenberger Company**

(a)

(b)

(c)

(d)

(e)

Name

Section

Date

**Problem 8-3B**

**Sandy Hake Company**

(a), (b), and (c)

General Journal

| | Date | Account Titles and Explanation | Ref. | Debit | Credit | |
|---|---|---|---|---|---|---|
| 1 | (a) | | | | | 1 |
| 2 | | | | | | 2 |
| 3 | | | | | | 3 |
| 4 | | | | | | 4 |
| 5 | | | | | | 5 |
| 6 | (b) | | | | | 6 |
| 7 | | | | | | 7 |
| 8 | | | | | | 8 |
| 9 | | | | | | 9 |
| 10 | | | | | | 10 |
| 11 | | | | | | 11 |
| 12 | | | | | | 12 |
| 13 | | | | | | 13 |
| 14 | | | | | | 14 |
| 15 | | | | | | 15 |
| 16 | | | | | | 16 |
| 17 | | | | | | 17 |
| 18 | | | | | | 18 |
| 19 | (c) | | | | | 19 |
| 20 | | | | | | 20 |
| 21 | | | | | | 21 |
| 22 | | | | | | 22 |

(a) and (b)

Bad Debts Expense

| | Date | Explanation | Ref. | Debit | Credit | Balance | |
|---|---|---|---|---|---|---|---|
| 1 | | | | | | | 1 |
| 2 | | | | | | | 2 |
| 3 | | | | | | | 3 |

Allowance for Doubtful Accounts

| | Date | Explanation | Ref. | Debit | Credit | Balance | |
|---|---|---|---|---|---|---|---|
| 1 | | | | | | | 1 |
| 2 | | | | | | | 2 |
| 3 | | | | | | | 3 |
| 4 | | | | | | | 4 |
| 5 | | | | | | | 5 |
| 6 | | | | | | | 6 |
| 7 | | | | | | | 7 |
| 8 | | | | | | | 8 |

Name | **Problem 8-4B**

Section

Date | **Lexington Company**

(a)

(b)

(c)

(d)

(e)

Name

Section

Date

**Problem 8-5B**

**Cheryl French Company**

(a)

General Journal

| Date | Account Titles and Explanation | Ref. | Debit | Credit |
|---|---|---|---|---|

Name  **Problem 8-5B Concluded**

Section

Date  **Cheryl French Company**

(b)

Notes Receivable

| Date | Explanation | Ref. | Debit | Credit | Balance |
|---|---|---|---|---|---|
| | | | | | |
| | | | | | |
| | | | | | |
| | | | | | |
| | | | | | |

Accounts Receivable

| Date | Explanation | Ref. | Debit | Credit | Balance |
|---|---|---|---|---|---|
| | | | | | |
| | | | | | |
| | | | | | |
| | | | | | |
| | | | | | |

Interest Receivable

| Date | Explanation | Ref. | Debit | Credit | Balance |
|---|---|---|---|---|---|
| | | | | | |
| | | | | | |
| | | | | | |
| | | | | | |
| | | | | | |
| | | | | | |

(c)

CHERYL FRENCH COMPANY
Balance Sheet (Partial)
October 31, 1999

| | | |
|---|---|---|
| Assets | | |
| Current Assets | | |
| | | |
| | | |
| | | |
| | | |
| | | |
| | | |

Name **Problem 8-6B**

Section

Date **Paul Gleason Company**

General Journal

| | Date | Account Titles and Explanation | Ref. | Debit | Credit | |
|---|---|---|---|---|---|---|
| 1 | | | | | | 1 |
| 2 | | | | | | 2 |
| 3 | | | | | | 3 |
| 4 | | | | | | 4 |
| 5 | | | | | | 5 |
| 6 | | | | | | 6 |
| 7 | | | | | | 7 |
| 8 | | | | | | 8 |
| 9 | | | | | | 9 |
| 10 | | | | | | 10 |
| 11 | | | | | | 11 |
| 12 | | | | | | 12 |
| 13 | | | | | | 13 |
| 14 | | | | | | 14 |
| 15 | | | | | | 15 |
| 16 | | | | | | 16 |
| 17 | | | | | | 17 |
| 18 | | | | | | 18 |
| 19 | | | | | | 19 |
| 20 | | | | | | 20 |
| 21 | | | | | | 21 |
| 22 | | | | | | 22 |
| 23 | | | | | | 23 |
| 24 | | | | | | 24 |
| 25 | | | | | | 25 |
| 26 | | | | | | 26 |
| 27 | | | | | | 27 |
| 28 | | | | | | 28 |
| 29 | | | | | | 29 |
| 30 | | | | | | 30 |
| 31 | | | | | | 31 |
| 32 | | | | | | 32 |
| 33 | | | | | | 33 |
| 34 | | | | | | 34 |
| 35 | | | | | | 35 |
| 36 | | | | | | 36 |
| 37 | | | | | | 37 |
| 38 | | | | | | 38 |
| 39 | | | | | | 39 |
| 40 | | | | | | 40 |

Name _______________ **Chapter 8 Financial Reporting Problem**

Section _______________

Date _______________ **SCH Company**

(a)

SCH COMPANY

Accounts Receivable Aging Schedule

May 31, 2000

| | Proportion of Total % | Amount in Category | Probability of Non-Collection % | Estimated Uncollectible Amount |
|---|---|---|---|---|
| Not yet due | | | | |
| | | | | |
| Less than 30 days past due | | | | |
| | | | | |
| 30 to 60 days past due | | | | |
| | | | | |
| 61 to 120 days past due | | | | |
| | | | | |
| 121 to 180 days past due | | | | |
| | | | | |
| Over 180 days past due | | | | |
| | | | | |
| Totals | | | | |
| | | | | |
| | | | | |

SCH COMPANY

Analysis of Allowance for Doubtful Accounts

May 31, 2000

(c)

| 1. Steps to Improve Accounts Receivable Collection | 2. Risks and Costs Involved |
|---|---|

 

Name

Section

Date

**Chapter 8 Comparative Analysis Problem**

**Kellogg vs. General Mills**

| (a) | Kellogg | General Mills |
|---|---|---|
| | | |
| (1) Accounts receivable turnover ratio | | |
| | | |
| (2) Average receivables collection period | | |
| | | |

(b)

(a)

(b)

(c)

(d)

Name ______________________ **Chapter 8 Group Decision Case**

Section ______________________

Date ______________________ **Somonauk Fashions**

| | 1999 | 1998 | 1997 |
|---|---|---|---|
| (a) Net credit sales | | | |
| Credit and collection expenses | | | |
| Total expenses as a percentage of net credit sales | | | |
| (b) Average accounts receivable | | | |
| Investment earnings | | | |
| Net expenses as a percentage of net credit sales | | | |

(c)

Name

Section

Date

**REAL-WORLD FOCUS** Art World Industries, Inc.

1.

2.

3.

**ETHICS CASE** Jacket Co.

(a)

(b)

(c)

Name

Section

Date

Name

Section

Date

Name

Section

Date

Name

Section

Date

Name

Section

Date

#1

#2

Name

Section

Date

**Exercise 9-**

**Mexico Company**

MEXICO COMPANY

Income Statement

For the Month Ended January 31, 1999

Name

Section

Date

| | |
|---|---|
| **#4** Ending inventory—physical count | 297,000 |

FIFO

Proof:

LIFO

Proof:

Name

Section

Date

**Exercise 9-6**

**Luxembourg Company**

(a) (1) FIFO

(2) LIFO

(b)

(c)

Name

Section

Date

#7 (a)

(b)

(c)

| #9 | 1999 | 2000 |
|---|---|---|

Name

Section

Date

**Exercise 9-8**

**China Camera Shop**

| | Inventory Items | Total Cost | Market | Lower of Cost or Market by (a) Individual Items | Lower of Cost or Market by (b) Major Categories | Lower of Cost or Market by (c) Total Inventory | |
|---|---|---|---|---|---|---|---|
| 1 | | | | | | | 1 |
| 2 | Cameras | | | | | | 2 |
| 3 | | | | | | | 3 |
| 4 | Minolta | | | | | | 4 |
| 5 | | | | | | | 5 |
| 6 | Canon | | | | | | 6 |
| 7 | | | | | | | 7 |
| 8 | Total | | | | | | 8 |
| 9 | | | | | | | 9 |
| 10 | | | | | | | 10 |
| 11 | Light Meters | | | | | | 11 |
| 12 | | | | | | | 12 |
| 13 | Vivitar | | | | | | 13 |
| 14 | | | | | | | 14 |
| 15 | Kodak | | | | | | 15 |
| 16 | | | | | | | 16 |
| 17 | Total | | | | | | 17 |
| 18 | | | | | | | 18 |
| 19 | | | | | | | 19 |
| 20 | Total Inventory | | | | | | 20 |
| 21 | | | | | | | 21 |
| 22 | | | | | | | 22 |

Name                                                                 **Exercise 9-10**

Section

Date                                                                 **Zurich Watch Company**

| | 1999 | 2000 |
|---|---|---|
| (a) | | |

(b)

(c)

Name

Section

Date

**Exercise 9-1**

**Linda Wasicsko Corporatio**

| | 1997 | 1998 | 1999 |
|---|---|---|---|
| Inventory turnover | | | |
| ratio | | | |
| Days in inventory | | | |
| Gross profit rate | | | |

Name *Exercises 9-12 to 9-13

Section

Date

**#12**

(a)

(b)

**#13**

| | Women's Department | | Men's Department | |
|---|---|---|---|---|
| | Cost | Retail | Cost | Retail |
| | | | | |
| Cost-to-retail ratio | | | | |
| | | | | |
| Estimated cost of ending inventory | | | | |

 

Name

Section

Date

***Exercise 9-14**

**Morocco Appliance Company**

FIFO

| Date | Purchases | Sales | Balance |
|---|---|---|---|
| | | | |
| | | | |
| | | | |
| | | | |
| | | | |
| | | | |
| | | | |
| | | | |
| | | | |
| | | | |

LIFO

| Date | Purchases | Sales | Balance |
|---|---|---|---|
| | | | |
| | | | |
| | | | |
| | | | |
| | | | |
| | | | |
| | | | |
| | | | |
| | | | |
| | | | |

AVERAGE COST

| Date | Purchases | Sales | Balance |
|---|---|---|---|
| | | | |
| | | | |
| | | | |
| | | | |
| | | | |
| | | | |
| | | | |
| | | | |
| | | | |
| | | | |

Name | **Problem 9-1A**

Section

Date | **Chi Chi's Pro Shop**

(a) General Journal

| Date | Account Titles and Explanation | Ref. | Debit | Credit |
|---|---|---|---|---|

(a) (Continued)

General Journal

| | Date | Account Titles and Explanation | Ref. | Debit | Credit | |
|---|---|---|---|---|---|---|
| 1 | | | | | | 1 |
| 2 | | | | | | 2 |
| 3 | | | | | | 3 |
| 4 | | | | | | 4 |
| 5 | | | | | | 5 |
| 6 | | | | | | 6 |

(b)

Cash No. 101

| Date | Explanation | Ref. | Debit | Credit | Balance |
|---|---|---|---|---|---|
| | | | | | |
| | | | | | |
| | | | | | |
| | | | | | |
| | | | | | |
| | | | | | |
| | | | | | |

Accounts Receivable No. 112

| Date | Explanation | Ref. | Debit | Credit | Balance |
|---|---|---|---|---|---|
| | | | | | |
| | | | | | |
| | | | | | |
| | | | | | |
| | | | | | |

Merchandise Inventory No. 120

| Date | Explanation | Ref. | Debit | Credit | Balance |
|---|---|---|---|---|---|
| | | | | | |
| | | | | | |

Accounts Payable No. 201

| Date | Explanation | Ref. | Debit | Credit | Balance |
|---|---|---|---|---|---|
| | | | | | |
| | | | | | |
| | | | | | |
| | | | | | |
| | | | | | |
| | | | | | |
| | | | | | |

(b)

C. Lopez, Capital — No. 301

| Date | Explanation | Ref. | Debit | Credit | Balance |
|---|---|---|---|---|---|
| | | | | | |
| | | | | | |

Sales — No. 401

| Date | Explanation | Ref. | Debit | Credit | Balance |
|---|---|---|---|---|---|
| | | | | | |
| | | | | | |
| | | | | | |
| | | | | | |

Sales Returns and Allowances — No. 412

| Date | Explanation | Ref. | Debit | Credit | Balance |
|---|---|---|---|---|---|
| | | | | | |
| | | | | | |

Purchases — No. 510

| Date | Explanation | Ref. | Debit | Credit | Balance |
|---|---|---|---|---|---|
| | | | | | |
| | | | | | |
| | | | | | |

Purchase Returns and Allowances — No. 512

| Date | Explanation | Ref. | Debit | Credit | Balance |
|---|---|---|---|---|---|
| | | | | | |
| | | | | | |
| | | | | | |

Purchase Discounts — No. 514

| Date | Explanation | Ref. | Debit | Credit | Balance |
|---|---|---|---|---|---|
| | | | | | |
| | | | | | |
| | | | | | |

Freight-in — No. 516

| Date | Explanation | Ref. | Debit | Credit | Balance |
|---|---|---|---|---|---|
| | | | | | |
| | | | | | |

(c)

CHI CHI'S PRO SHOP
Trial Balance
April 30,1999

| | Debit | Credit |
|---|---|---|

(d)

CHI CHI'S PRO SHOP
Income Statement (Partial)
For the Month Ended April 30, 1999

Name **Problem 9-2A**

Section

Date **Asian Department Store**

ASIAN DEPARTMENT STORE
Income Statement
For the Month Ended November 30, 1999

 

Name
Section
Date

**Problem 9-2A Concluded**

**Asian Department Store**

ASIAN DEPARTMENT STORE
Income Statement (Continued)
For the Month Ended November 30, 1999

| | | |
|---|---|---|
| 1 | | |
| 2 | | |
| 3 | | |
| 4 | | |
| 5 | | |
| 6 | | |
| 7 | | |
| 8 | | |
| 9 | | |
| 10 | | |
| 11 | | |
| 12 | | |
| 13 | | |
| 14 | | |
| 15 | | |
| 16 | | |
| 17 | | |
| 18 | | |
| 19 | | |
| 20 | | |

Name **Problem 9-3A**

Section

Date **Europe Company**

(a)

| COST OF GOODS AVAILABLE FOR SALE | | | | |
|---|---|---|---|---|
| Date | Explanation | Units | Unit Cost | Total Cost |

(b)

FIFO

(1) Ending Inventory

| Date | Units | x | Unit Cost | = | Total Cost |
|---|---|---|---|---|---|

(2) Cost of Goods Sold

Proof of Cost of Goods Sold

| Date | Units | x | Unit Cost | = | Total Cost |
|---|---|---|---|---|---|

LIFO

(1) Ending Inventory

| Date | Units | x | Unit Cost | = | Total Cost |
|---|---|---|---|---|---|

(2) Cost of Goods Sold

(b) (Continued) and (c)

(b) Proof of Cost of Goods Sold

| Date | Units | × | Unit Cost | = | Total Cost |
|---|---|---|---|---|---|

AVERAGE COST

(1) Ending Inventory

(2) Cost of Goods Sold

| Units | × | Unit Cost | = | Total Cost |
|---|---|---|---|---|

Proof of Cost of Goods Sold

(c)

| | FIFO | LIFO | Average Cost |
|---|---|---|---|

Name **Problem 9-4A**

Section

Date **African Co.**

(a)

AFRICAN CO.
Condensed Income Statements
For the Year Ended December 31, 1999

| | FIFO | LIFO |
|---|---|---|
| | | |

(b) (1)

(2)

(3)

(4)

(5)

(b) (Continued) Letter

Name ***Problem 9-5A**

Section

Date **Australia Company**

(a) November

(b) Estimated Inventory Loss

Name ***Problem 9-6A**

Section

Date **French's Book Store**

(a)

| | Hardcovers | | Paperbacks | |
|---|---|---|---|---|
| | Cost | Retail | Cost | Retail |
| Cost-to-retail ratio: | | | | |
| Estimated ending inventory at cost: | | | | |

(b)

| |
|---|
| Hardcovers: |
| Paperbacks: |

Name

Section

Date

***Problem 9-7A**

**Save-Mart Center**

(a) (1)

| FIFO | | | |
|---|---|---|---|
| Date | Purchases | Sales | Balance |
| | | | |

(2)

| AVERAGE COST | | | |
|---|---|---|---|
| Date | Purchases | Sales | Balance |
| | | | |

Name

Section

Date

***Problem 9-7A Concluded**

**Save-Mart Center**

(a) (Continued)

(3)

| LIFO | | | |
|---|---|---|---|
| Date | Purchases | Sales | Balance |

(b)

(1)

(2)

Name  **Problem 9-1B**

Section

Date  **B. J.'s Tennis Shop**

(a) General Journal

| Date | Account Titles and Explanation | Ref. | Debit | Credit |
| --- | --- | --- | --- | --- |
| | | | | |

Name
Section
Date



(a) (Continued)

General Journal

| | Date | Account Titles and Explanation | Ref. | Debit | Credit | |
|---|---|---|---|---|---|---|
| 1 | | | | | | 1 |
| 2 | | | | | | 2 |
| 3 | | | | | | 3 |
| 4 | | | | | | 4 |
| 5 | | | | | | 5 |
| 6 | | | | | | 6 |
| 7 | | | | | | 7 |
| 8 | | | | | | 8 |
| 9 | | | | | | 9 |

(b)

Cash — No. 101

| Date | Explanation | Ref. | Debit | Credit | Balance |
|---|---|---|---|---|---|
| | | | | | |

Accounts Receivable — No. 112

| Date | Explanation | Ref. | Debit | Credit | Balance |
|---|---|---|---|---|---|
| | | | | | |

Merchandise Inventory — No. 120

| Date | Explanation | Ref. | Debit | Credit | Balance |
|---|---|---|---|---|---|
| | | | | | |

Name
Section
Date

**Problem 9-1B Continued**

**B. J.'s Tennis Shop**

(b) (Continued)

Accounts Payable — No. 201

| Date | Explanation | Ref. | Debit | Credit | Balance |
|---|---|---|---|---|---|
| | | | | | |
| | | | | | |
| | | | | | |
| | | | | | |
| | | | | | |
| | | | | | |

B. J. Evert, Capital — No. 301

| Date | Explanation | Ref. | Debit | Credit | Balance |
|---|---|---|---|---|---|
| | | | | | |
| | | | | | |

Sales — No. 401

| Date | Explanation | Ref. | Debit | Credit | Balance |
|---|---|---|---|---|---|
| | | | | | |
| | | | | | |
| | | | | | |
| | | | | | |

Sales Returns and Allowances — No. 412

| Date | Explanation | Ref. | Debit | Credit | Balance |
|---|---|---|---|---|---|
| | | | | | |
| | | | | | |

Purchases — No. 501

| Date | Explanation | Ref. | Debit | Credit | Balance |
|---|---|---|---|---|---|
| | | | | | |
| | | | | | |
| | | | | | |
| | | | | | |

Purchase Returns and Allowances — No. 512

| Date | Explanation | Ref. | Debit | Credit | Balance |
|---|---|---|---|---|---|
| | | | | | |
| | | | | | |
| | | | | | |

Name

Section

Date

**Problem 9-1B Continued**

**B. J.'s Tennis Shop**

(b) (Continued)

Purchase Discounts — No. 514

| Date | Explanation | Ref. | Debit | Credit | Balance |
|---|---|---|---|---|---|
| | | | | | |
| | | | | | |
| | | | | | |

Freight-in — No. 516

| Date | Explanation | Ref. | Debit | Credit | Balance |
|---|---|---|---|---|---|
| | | | | | |
| | | | | | |
| | | | | | |

(c)

B. J.'S TENNIS SHOP
Trial Balance
April 30, 1999

| | | Debit | Credit | |
|---|---|---|---|---|
| 1 | | | | 1 |
| 2 | | | | 2 |
| 3 | | | | 3 |
| 4 | | | | 4 |
| 5 | | | | 5 |
| 6 | | | | 6 |
| 7 | | | | 7 |
| 8 | | | | 8 |
| 9 | | | | 9 |
| 10 | | | | 10 |
| 11 | | | | 11 |
| 12 | | | | 12 |
| 13 | | | | 13 |
| 14 | | | | 14 |

Name

Section

Date





(b)

B. J.'S TENNIS SHOP
Income Statement (Partial)
For the Month Ended April 30, 1999

Name

Section

Date

**Problem 9-2B**

**Austrian Department Store**

AUSTRIAN DEPARTMENT STORE
Income Statement
For the Year Ended December 31, 1999

AUSTRIAN DEPARTMENT STORE
Income Statement (Continued)
For the Year Ended December 31, 1999

Name | **Problem 9-3B**
Section
Date | **Europe Company**

(a)

| COST OF GOODS AVAILABLE FOR SALE | | | | |
|---|---|---|---|---|
| Date | Explanation | Units | Unit Cost | Total Cost |
| | | | | |
| | | | | |
| | | | | |
| | | | | |
| | | | | |
| | | | | |
| | | | | |

(b)

FIFO

(1) Ending Inventory | (2) Cost of Goods Sold

| Date | Units | x | Unit Cost | = | Total Cost |
|---|---|---|---|---|---|

Proof of Cost of Goods Sold

| Date | Units | x | Unit Cost | = | Total Cost |
|---|---|---|---|---|---|

LIFO

(1) Ending Inventory | (2) Cost of Goods Sold

| Date | Units | x | Unit Cost | = | Total Cost |
|---|---|---|---|---|---|

(b) (Continued) and (c)

Proof of Cost of Goods Sold

| Date | Units | × | Unit Cost | = | Total Cost |
|---|---|---|---|---|---|

AVERAGE COST

(1) Ending Inventory

(2) Cost of Goods Sold

| Units | × | Unit Cost | = | Total Cost |
|---|---|---|---|---|

Proof of Cost of Goods Sold

(c)

| | FIFO | LIFO | Average Cost |
|---|---|---|---|

Name

Section

Date

**Problem 9-4[cut off]**

**India Co[cut off]**

(a)

INDIA CO.
Condensed Income Statements
For the Year Ended December 31, 1999

| | FIFO | LIFO |
|---|---|---|
| | | |

(b) (1)

(2)

(3)

(4)

(5)

Name

Section

Date

*Problem 9-5B

Tibet Company

(a)

February

(b)

Estimated Inventory Loss

Name

Section

Date

***Problem 9-6B**

**Martinez Department Store**

(a)

| | Sporting Goods | | Jewelry and Cosmetics | |
|---|---|---|---|---|
| | Cost | Retail | Cost | Retail |
| | | | | |
| Cost-to-retail ratio: | | | | |
| | | | | |
| Estimated ending inventory at cost: | | | | |
| | | | | |

(b)

| |
|---|
| Sporting Goods: |
| |
| |
| Jewelry and Cosmetics: |
| |
| |

Name

Section

Date

***Problem 9-7B**

**Japanese Department Store**

(a) (1)

| FIFO | | | |
|---|---|---|---|
| Date | Purchases | Sales | Balance |

(2)

| AVERAGE COST | | | |
|---|---|---|---|
| Date | Purchases | Sales | Balance |

Name

Section

Date



(a) (Continued) (3)

| LIFO | | | |
|---|---|---|---|
| Date | Purchases | Sales | Balance |

(b)

(1)

(2)

Name

Section

Date

## Chapter 9 Financial Reporting Problem

## Kellogg Company

(a)

(b)

(c)

(d)

Name

Section

Date

**Kellogg vs. General Mills**

| (a) | Kellogg | General Mills |
|---|---|---|
| Inventory turnover ratio: | | |
| Average days to sell inventory: | | |

(b)

Name

Section

Date



**Nike and Reebok**

(a), (b), and (c)

(a)

(b)

(c)

Name

Section

Date



(d)

| | Nike | Reebok |
|---|---|---|
| Inventory turnover ratio: | | |
| Average days to sell inventory: | | |

Name

Section

Date

**Chapter 9 Decision Case**

**Gibson Company**

(a) (1) Sales

(2) Purchases

(b)

| | 1997 | 1996 |
|---|---|---|

(c)

Name

Section

Date

**REAL-WORLD FOCUS** General Motors Corporation

(a)

(b)

(c)

**ETHICS CASE** Lonergan Wholesale Company

(a)

(b)

(c)

Name

Section

Date

Name

Section

Date

Name

Section

Date

Name

Section

Date

Name **Exercises 10-1 to 10-2**

Section

Date

**#1**

**#2**

Name

Section

Date



**#3**

(a)

(b)

| Computation | Annual Depreciation Expense | End of Year: Accumulated Depreciation | End of Year: Book Value |
|---|---|---|---|

**#4**

(1)

(2)

(3)

Name

Section

Date

**Exercises 10-5 to 10-6**

#5

#6

Name

Section

Date

**Exercise 10-7**

**White Cloud Co. and Nelle Inc.**

1.

2.

Name

Section

Date

**Exercise 10-8**

**Wind Company and Sun Company**

Wind Company:

Sun Company:

Name

Section

Date



**#9** (a) Peru's Delivery Company:

(b) Brazil's Express Delivery:

**#13**

Name **Exercises 10-10 to 10-11**

Section

Date

**#10**

(a)

(b)

**#11**

Name

Section

Date

**Exercise 10-12**

**Vail Company**

Ending balances, 12/31/99:

Name

Section

Date

**Problem 10-1A**

**Superior Company**

| Item | Land | Building | Other Accounts Amount | Other Accounts Account Titles |
|---|---|---|---|---|
| | | | | |
| 1. | | | | |
| | | | | |
| 2. | | | | |
| | | | | |
| 3. | | | | |
| | | | | |
| 4. | | | | |
| | | | | |
| 5. | | | | |
| | | | | |
| 6. | | | | |
| | | | | |
| 7. | | | | |
| | | | | |
| 8. | | | | |
| | | | | |
| 9. | | | | |
| | | | | |
| 10. | | | | |
| | | | | |
| | | | | |
| | | | | |
| | | | | |
| | | | | |

Name

Section

Date

**Problem 10-2A**

**Eric Company**

| Year | Computation | Cumulative, 12/31 |
|---|---|---|
| (a) | MACHINE 1 | |
| | | |
| 1996 | | |
| | | |
| 1997 | | |
| | | |
| 1998 | | |
| | | |
| 1999 | | |
| | | |
| | | |
| | MACHINE 2 | |
| | | |
| 1997 | | |
| | | |
| 1998 | | |
| | | |
| 1999 | | |
| | | |
| | | |
| | MACHINE 3 | |
| | | |
| 1999 | | |
| | | |
| | | |
| | | |
| | | |
| | | |
| | | |
| (b) | MACHINE 2 | Expense |
| | | |
| (1) 1997 | | |
| | | |
| (2) 1998 | | |
| | | |
| | | |
| | | |
| | | |
| | | |
| | | |

Name
Section
Date

**Problem 10-3A**

**Rose Company**

(a) and (b)

(a)

(b) (1)

(2)

| | Beginning-of-year Book Value | DDB Rate | Annual Depreciation Expense | Accumulated Depreciation |
|---|---|---|---|---|

Name

Section

Date



(b) (Continued) and (c)

(b) (3) Depreciation cost per unit:

| Year | Computation | Depreciation Expense |
|---|---|---|
| | | |
| 1999 | | |
| | | |
| 2000 | | |
| | | |
| 2001 | | |
| | | |
| 2002 | | |
| | | |
| 2003 | | |
| | | |

(c)

Name | **Problem 10-4A**

Section

Date | **Wallace Company**

(a) General Journal

| Date | Account Titles and Explanation | Ref. | Debit | Credit |
|---|---|---|---|---|

Name

Section

Date

**Problem 10-4A Continued**

**Wallace Company**

(a) (Continued) and (b) General Journal

| Date | Account Titles and Explanation | Ref. | Debit | Credit |
|---|---|---|---|---|
| (b) | | | | |

Name

Section

Date



**Wallace Company**

T-accounts for balance calculations

LAND

BUILDINGS

ACCUM. DEPRECIATION—BUILDINGS

EQUIPMENT

ACCUM. DEPRECIATION—EQUIP.

(c)

WALLACE COMPANY
Balance Sheet (Partial)
December 31, 2000

| | | |
|---|---|---|
| Assets | | |
| Plant Assets | | |
| | | |
| | | |
| | | |
| | | |
| | | |
| | | |
| | | |
| | | |
| | | |
| | | |

Name

Section

Date

**Problem 10-5A**

**Ghani Co.**

(a)—(d)

General Journal

| Date | Account Titles and Explanation | Ref. | Debit | Credit |
|---|---|---|---|---|
| (a) | | | | |
| (b) | | | | |
| (c) | | | | |
| (d) | | | | |

Name

Section

Date

**Problem 10-5A Concluded**

**Ghani Co.**

(d) (Continued) and (e)

General Journal

| Date | Account Titles and Explanation | Ref. | Debit | Credit |
|---|---|---|---|---|
| (d) | (Continued) | | | |
| (e) | | | | |

Name

Section

Date

**Problem 10-6A**

**El-Gazzar Company**

(a)

(b)

(c)

(d)

Name

Section

Date

**Problem 10-7A**

**Baird Corporation**

General Journal

| | Account Titles and Explanation | Debit | Credit |
|---|---|---|---|
| 1. | | | |
| | | | |
| | | | |
| | | | |
| | | | |
| | | | |
| | | | |
| | | | |
| | | | |
| | | | |
| 2. | | | |
| | | | |
| | | | |
| | | | |
| | | | |
| | | | |
| | | | |
| | | | |
| | | | |
| | | | |

Name

Section

Date

**Problem 10-8A**

**Croix Corp. and Rye Corp.**

| | Croix Corp. | Rye Corp. |
|---|---|---|
| (a) | | |
| (1) Average age of plant assests | | |
| | | |
| (2) Average useful life of plant assets | | |
| | | |
| (3) Asset turnover ratio | | |

(b)

Name

Section

Date

**Problem 10-1B**

**Bob Duran Company**

| Item | Land | Building | Other Accounts: Amount | Other Accounts: Account Titles |
|---|---|---|---|---|
| 1. | | | | |
| 2. | | | | |
| 3. | | | | |
| 4. | | | | |
| 5. | | | | |
| 6. | | | | |
| 7. | | | | |
| 8. | | | | |
| 9. | | | | |
| 10. | | | | |

Name

Section

Date

**Problem 10-2B**

**Lakeshore Transporatio**

| Year | Computation | Cumulative, 12/31 |
|---|---|---|
| (a) | BUS 1 | |
| | | |
| 1997 | | |
| | | |
| 1998 | | |
| | | |
| 1999 | | |
| | | |
| | | |
| | | |
| | | |
| | BUS 2 | |
| | | |
| 1997 | | |
| | | |
| 1998 | | |
| | | |
| 1999 | | |
| | | |
| | | |
| | BUS 3 | |
| | | |
| 1998 | | |
| | | |
| 1999 | | |
| | | |
| | | |
| | | |
| | | |
| (b) | BUS 2 | Expense |
| | | |
| (1) 1997 | | |
| | | |
| (2) 1998 | | |
| | | |
| | | |
| | | |
| | | |
| | | |
| | | |

Name

Section

Date

**Problem 10-3B**

**Axel Company**

(a) and (b)

(a)

(b) (1)

| (2) | Beginning-of-year Book Value | DDB Rate | Annual Depreciation Expense | Accumulated Depreciation |
|---|---|---|---|---|
| | | | | |

Name

Section

Date

**Problem 10-3B Concluded**

**Axel Company**

(b) (Continued) and (c)

(b) (3) Depreciation cost per unit:

| Year | Computation | Depreciation Expense |
|---|---|---|
| 1999 | | |
| 2000 | | |
| 2001 | | |
| 2002 | | |

(c)

Name

Section

Date

**Problem 10-4B**

**Los Alamos Company**

(a) General Journal

| Date | Account Titles and Explanation | Ref. | Debit | Credit |
|---|---|---|---|---|

Name

Section

Date

**Problem 10-4B Continued**

**Los Alamos Company**

(a) (Continued) and (b)

General Journal

| Date | Account Titles and Explanation | Ref. | Debit | Credit |
|---|---|---|---|---|
| (b) | | | | |

Name
Section
Date

**Problem 10-4B Concluded**

**Los Alamos Company**

T-accounts for balance calculations

LAND

BUILDINGS

ACCUM. DEPRECIATION—BUILDINGS

EQUIPMENT

ACCUM. DEPRECIATION—EQUIP.

(c)

LOS ALAMOS COMPANY
Balance Sheet (Partial)
December 31, 2000

Name Problem 10-5

Section

Date Chon Co

(a)—(d) General Journal

| Date | Account Titles and Explanation | Ref. | Debit | Credit |
|---|---|---|---|---|
| (a) | | | | |
| (b) | | | | |
| (c) | | | | |
| (d) | | | | |

 

Name **Problem 10-5B Concluded**

Section

Date **Chon Co.**

(d) (Continued) and (e) General Journal

| Date | Account Titles and Explanation | Ref. | Debit | Credit |
|---|---|---|---|---|
| (d) | (Continued) | | | |
| (e) | | | | |

Name

Section

Date

**Problem 10-6**

**De Paul Compan**

(a)

(b)

(c)

Name **Problem 10-7B**

Section

Date **Coker Company**

General Journal

| | Account Titles and Explanation | Debit | Credit |
|---|---|---|---|
| 1. | | | |
| | | | |
| | | | |
| | | | |
| | | | |
| | | | |
| | | | |
| | | | |
| | | | |
| | | | |
| 2. | | | |
| | | | |
| | | | |
| | | | |
| | | | |
| | | | |
| | | | |
| | | | |
| | | | |
| | | | |

Name

Section

Date

**Problem 10-8**

**Reggie Corp. and Newman Cor**

| (a) | Reggie Corp. | Newman Corp. |
| --- | --- | --- |
| (1) Average age of plant assests | | |
| (2) Average useful life of plant assets | | |
| (3) Asset turnover ratio | | |

(b)

Name

Section

Date

**Chapter 10 Financial Reporting Problem**

**Kellogg Company**

(a)

(b)

(c)

(d)

(e)

(f)

(g)

Name

Section

Date

| (a) | Kellogg | General Mills |
| --- | --- | --- |
| (1) Average life of plant assets | | |
| (2) Average age of plant assets | | |
| (3) Asset turnover ratio | | |

(b)

Name

Section

Date



**Boeing vs. McDonnell Douglas**

(a)

(b)

(c)

(d)

Name

Section

Date



(a)

(b)

(c)

(d)

 

Name

Section

Date

## Fresno Company and Auburn Company

(a) Fresno Company — Straight-line method

Auburn Company — Double-declining-balance method

| Year | Asset | Computation | Annual Depreciation | Accumulated Depreciation |
|---|---|---|---|---|
| 1997 | Building | | | |
| | Equipment | | | |
| | | | | |
| 1998 | Building | | | |
| | Equipment | | | |
| | | | | |
| 1999 | Building | | | |
| | Equipment | | | |

(b)

| Year | Fresno Co. Net Income | Auburn Co. Net Income as Adjusted | Computations for Auburn Company |
|---|---|---|---|
| | | | |
| 1997 | | | |
| | | | |
| 1998 | | | |
| | | | |
| 1999 | | | |
| | | | |
| Total | | | |

(c)

Name

Section

Date



| **REAL-WORLD FOCUS** | Clark Equipment Company |
|---|---|
| (a) | |
| (b) | |
| (c) | |

Name

Section

Date

**ETHICS CASE** Finney Container Company

(a)

(b)

(c)

Old Estimates

Revised Estimates

Name

Section

Date

Name

Section

Date



| | | | | | |
|---|---|---|---|---|---|
| 1 | | | | | 1 |
| 2 | | | | | 2 |
| 3 | | | | | 3 |
| 4 | | | | | 4 |
| 5 | | | | | 5 |
| 6 | | | | | 6 |
| 7 | | | | | 7 |
| 8 | | | | | 8 |
| 9 | | | | | 9 |
| 10 | | | | | 10 |
| 11 | | | | | 11 |
| 12 | | | | | 12 |
| 13 | | | | | 13 |
| 14 | | | | | 14 |
| 15 | | | | | 15 |
| 16 | | | | | 16 |
| 17 | | | | | 17 |
| 18 | | | | | 18 |
| 19 | | | | | 19 |
| 20 | | | | | 20 |
| 21 | | | | | 21 |
| 22 | | | | | 22 |
| 23 | | | | | 23 |
| 24 | | | | | 24 |
| 25 | | | | | 25 |
| 26 | | | | | 26 |
| 27 | | | | | 27 |
| 28 | | | | | 28 |
| 29 | | | | | 29 |
| 30 | | | | | 30 |
| 31 | | | | | 31 |
| 32 | | | | | 32 |
| 33 | | | | | 33 |
| 34 | | | | | 34 |
| 35 | | | | | 35 |
| 36 | | | | | 36 |
| 37 | | | | | 37 |
| 38 | | | | | 38 |
| 39 | | | | | 39 |
| 40 | | | | | 40 |

Name

Section

Date

Name

Section

Date

**Exercises 11-1 to 11-3**

**#1**

**#2** Jardine Company

Lim Company

**#3**

Name

Section

Date

#4 (a)

(b)

(c)

#5 (a)

(b)

Name

Section

Date

**#6**

**#7** (a)

(b)

Name

Section

Date



**#8** (a)

(b)

**#9** K. Ostman

B. Sailors

C. Leggett

R. Ryan

Name **Exercise 11-10**

Section

Date **Egypt Company**

(a)

EGYPT COMPANY
Payroll Register
For the Week Ending January 31

| | Employee | Total Hours | Earnings: Regular | Overtime | Gross Pay | |
|---|---|---|---|---|---|---|
| 1 | S. Rudo | | | | | 1 |
| 2 | | | | | | 2 |
| 3 | N. Siena | | | | | 3 |
| 4 | | | | | | 4 |
| 5 | V. Ruble | | | | | 5 |
| 6 | | | | | | 6 |
| 7 | Totals | | | | | 7 |

(a) Continued

EGYPT COMPANY
Payroll Register (continued)
For the Week Ending January 31

| | | Deductions: FICA Taxes | Federal Income Taxes | Health Insurance | Total | Net Pay | |
|---|---|---|---|---|---|---|---|
| 1 | Rudo | | | | | | 1 |
| 2 | | | | | | | 2 |
| 3 | Siena | | | | | | 3 |
| 4 | | | | | | | 4 |
| 5 | Ruble | | | | | | 5 |
| 6 | | | | | | | 6 |
| 7 | Totals | | | | | | 7 |

(b) General Journal

| | Date | | Debit | Credit | |
|---|---|---|---|---|---|
| 1 | | | | | 1 |
| 2 | | | | | 2 |
| 3 | | | | | 3 |
| 4 | | | | | 4 |
| 5 | | | | | 5 |
| 6 | | | | | 6 |
| 7 | | | | | 7 |
| 8 | | | | | 8 |
| 9 | | | | | 9 |
| 10 | | | | | 10 |
| 11 | | | | | 11 |
| 12 | | | | | 12 |

**Exercises 11-11 to 11-13**

Name

Section

Date

#11 (a)

(b)

#12

#13

Name

Section

Date

**Problem 11-1A**

**Calcutta Company**

(a)

General Journal

| Date | Account Titles and Explanation | Ref. | Debit | Credit |
|---|---|---|---|---|

Name Problem 11-1A Concluded

Section

Date Calcutta Company

(b)

General Journal

| | Date | Account Titles and Explanation | Ref. | Debit | Credit | |
|---|---|---|---|---|---|---|
| 1 | | Adjusting Entries | | | | 1 |
| 2 | | | | | | 2 |
| 3 | | | | | | 3 |
| 4 | | | | | | 4 |
| 5 | | | | | | 5 |
| 6 | | | | | | 6 |
| 7 | | | | | | 7 |
| 8 | | | | | | 8 |
| 9 | | | | | | 9 |
| 10 | | | | | | 10 |
| 11 | | | | | | 11 |
| 12 | | | | | | 12 |
| 13 | | | | | | 13 |
| 14 | | | | | | 14 |
| 15 | | | | | | 15 |

(c)

CALCUTTA COMPANY
Balance Sheet (Partial)
January 31, 1999

| | | | | |
|---|---|---|---|---|
| 1 | Liabiliites and Owner's Equity | | | 1 |
| 2 | Current liabilities | | | 2 |
| 3 | | | | 3 |
| 4 | | | | 4 |
| 5 | | | | 5 |
| 6 | | | | 6 |
| 7 | | | | 7 |
| 8 | | | | 8 |
| 9 | | | | 9 |
| 10 | | | | 10 |
| 11 | | | | 11 |
| 12 | | | | 12 |
| 13 | | | | 13 |
| 14 | | | | 14 |
| 15 | | | | 15 |

 

Name

Section

Date

**Problem 11-2A**

**Villanova Drug Store**

(a)

VILLANOVA DRUG STORE

Payroll Register

For the Week Ended February 15, 1999

| Employee | Hours | Earnings | | | Deductions | | | | | Net Pay | Store Wages Exp. | Office Wages Exp. |
|---|---|---|---|---|---|---|---|---|---|---|---|---|
| | | Regular | Over-time | Gross Pay | FICA Taxes | Fed. Inc. Tax | State Inc. Tax | United Fund | Total | | | |
| O. Stratton | | | | | | | | | | | | |
| | | | | | | | | | | | | |
| E. Muse | | | | | | | | | | | | |
| | | | | | | | | | | | | |
| A. Horton | | | | | | | | | | | | |
| | | | | | | | | | | | | |
| F. Lupino | | | | | | | | | | | | |
| | | | | | | | | | | | | |
| Totals | | | | | | | | | | | | |
| | | | | | | | | | | | | |

Name

Section

Date

**Problem 11-2A Concluded**

**Villanova Drug Store**

(b)—(d) General Journal

| Date | Account Titles and Explanation | Ref. | Debit | Credit |
|---|---|---|---|---|
| (b) | | | | |
| (c) | | | | |
| (d) | | | | |

Name

Section

Date

**Problem 11-3A**

**Sanchez, Moscove, and Dominion Companies**

| (a) Weaknesses | (b) Recommended Procedures |
|---|---|
| 1. | |
| 2. | |
| 3. | |

ame

ection

ate

**Problem 11-4A**

**Carlos Costa Company**

General Journal

| Date | Account Titles and Explanation | Ref. | Debit | Credit |
|---|---|---|---|---|
| (a) | | | | |
| (b) | | | | |

Name

Section

Date

**Problem 11-5A**

**San Juan Electric Company**

(a) and (b)

General Journal

| Date | Account Titles and Explanation | Ref. | Debit | Credit |
|---|---|---|---|---|
| | | | | |

(c)

| Employee | Wages, Tips, Other Compensation | Federal Income Tax Withheld | State Income Tax Withheld | FICA Wages | FICA Tax Withheld |
|---|---|---|---|---|---|
| | | | | | |
| R. Cheng | | | | | |
| | | | | | |
| D. Craig | | | | | |

Name

Section

Date

**Problem 11-6A**

**Zimmer Company**

(a) General Journal

| Date | Account Titles and Explanation | Ref. | Debit | Credit |
|---|---|---|---|---|

(b) and (d)

NOTES PAYABLE

INTEREST PAYABLE

INTEREST EXPENSE

Total interest expense for the year is ______________.

(c)

ZIMMER COMPANY
Balance Sheet (Partial)
December 31

| | | | | |
|---|---|---|---|---|
| 1 | Liabilities and Owner's Equity | | | 1 |
| 2 | Current liabilities | | | 2 |
| 3 | | | | 3 |
| 4 | | | | 4 |
| 5 | | | | 5 |
| 6 | | | | 6 |
| 7 | | | | 7 |
| 8 | | | | 8 |

Name

Section

Date

**Problem 11-1B**

**El Paso Company**

(a) General Journal

| Date | Account Titles and Explanation | Ref. | Debit | Credit |
|---|---|---|---|---|
| | | | | |

(b) General Journal

| | Date | Account Titles and Explanation | Ref. | Debit | Credit |
|---|---|---|---|---|---|
| 1 | | Adjusting Entries | | | |
| 2 | | | | | |
| 3 | | | | | |
| 4 | | | | | |
| 5 | | | | | |
| 6 | | | | | |
| 7 | | | | | |
| 8 | | | | | |
| 9 | | | | | |
| 10 | | | | | |
| 11 | | | | | |
| 12 | | | | | |
| 13 | | | | | |
| 14 | | | | | |
| 15 | | | | | |

(c)

EL PASO COMPANY
Balance Sheet (Partial)
January 31, 1999

| | | | |
|---|---|---|---|
| 1 | Liabilities and Owner's Equity | | |
| 2 | Current liabilities | | |
| 3 | | | |
| 4 | | | |
| 5 | | | |
| 6 | | | |
| 7 | | | |
| 8 | | | |
| 9 | | | |
| 10 | | | |
| 11 | | | |
| 12 | | | |
| 13 | | | |
| 14 | | | |
| 15 | | | |

Section

Date

**UCLA Hardware**

(a)

UCLA HARDWARE

Payroll Register

For the Week Ended March 15, 1999

| Employee | Hours | Earnings | | | Deductions | | | | | Net Pay | Store Wages Exp. | Office Wages Exp. |
|---|---|---|---|---|---|---|---|---|---|---|---|---|
| | | Regular | Over-time | Gross Pay | FICA Taxes | Fed. Inc. Tax | State Inc. Tax | United Fund | Total | | | |
| J. Sanders | | | | | | | | | | | | |
| | | | | | | | | | | | | |
| S. Black | | | | | | | | | | | | |
| | | | | | | | | | | | | |
| D. Torres | | | | | | | | | | | | |
| | | | | | | | | | | | | |
| K. Kim | | | | | | | | | | | | |
| | | | | | | | | | | | | |
| Totals | | | | | | | | | | | | |
| | | | | | | | | | | | | |

Name

Section

Date

**Problem 11-2B Conclude**

**UCLA Hardwar**

(b)—(d) General Journal

| Date | Account Titles and Explanation | Ref. | Debit | Credit |
|---|---|---|---|---|
| (b) | | | | |
| (c) | | | | |
| (d) | | | | |

 

Name **Problem 11-3B**

Section

Date **Merced Sotera Company**

| (a) Weaknesses | (b) Recommended Procedures |
| --- | --- |
| 1. | |
| 2. | |
| 3. | |

 

Name **Problem 11-4**

Section

Date **Amora Compan**

General Journal

| Date | Account Titles and Explanation | Ref. | Debit | Credit |
|---|---|---|---|---|
| (a) | | | | |
| (b) | | | | |

Name | **Problem 11-5B**

Section

Date | **McMaster Electrical Repair Company**

(a) and (b)

General Journal

| Date | Account Titles and Explanation | Ref. | Debit | Credit |
|---|---|---|---|---|

(c)

| Employee | Wages, Tips, Other Compensation | Federal Income Tax Withheld | State Income Tax Withheld | FICA Wages | FICA Tax Withheld |
|---|---|---|---|---|---|
| | | | | | |
| J. Walker | | | | | |
| | | | | | |
| I. Zimmer | | | | | |
| | | | | | |

Name
Section
Date



**Kellogg Company**

(a)

(b)

(c)

| Type of current liability | Amount (in 000's) |
|---|---|
| | |

Name

Section

Date

**Chapter 11 Comparative Analysis Problem**

**Kellog vs. General Mills**

(a)

(b)

| | Kellogg | General Mills |
|---|---|---|
| (1) Working capital | | |
| (2) Current ratio | | |

(c)

Name

Section

Date

(a)

| | 1995 | 1994 |
|---|---|---|
| Working capital | | |
| | | |
| | | |
| | | |
| | | |
| | | |
| Current ratio | | |
| | | |
| | | |
| | | |
| | | |

(b)

(a)

SAUK PROCESSING COMPANY
Schedules: Comparative Employee Costs
Annual Estimates

| | HARRINGTON SERVICES, INC. | | | | | |
|---|---|---|---|---|---|---|
| | Month | Number of Employees | Days Worked | Daily Rate | Cost | |
| 1 | | | | | | 1 |
| 2 | | | | | | 2 |
| 3 | | | | | | 3 |
| 4 | | | | | | 4 |
| 5 | | | | | | 5 |
| 6 | | | | | | 6 |
| 7 | | | | | | 7 |
| 8 | | | | | | 8 |
| 9 | | | | | | 9 |
| 10 | | | | | | 10 |

| | PERMANENT EMPLOYEES | | | |
|---|---|---|---|---|
| 1 | Salaries | | | 1 |
| 2 | | | | 2 |
| 3 | Additional payroll costs | | | 3 |
| 4 | | | | 4 |
| 5 | | | | 5 |
| 6 | | | | 6 |
| 7 | | | | 7 |
| 8 | | | | 8 |
| 9 | | | | 9 |
| 10 | | | | 10 |

(b)

| | | |
|---|---|---|
| 1 | | 1 |
| 2 | | 2 |
| 3 | | 3 |
| 4 | | 4 |
| 5 | | 5 |
| 6 | | 6 |
| 7 | | 7 |
| 8 | | 8 |
| 9 | | 9 |
| 10 | | 10 |

**REAL-WORLD FOCUS** Capitol American Financial Corporation

**ETHICS CASE** Harry's Restaurant

 

Name

Section

Date

Name

Section

Date

Name

Section

Date

**Exercises 12-1 to 12-2**

**#1**

**#2**

Name

Section

Date

**#3**

**#4**

Name

Section

Date

#5

| | Current Period Costs | Total Estimated Costs | Percent Complete thru Current Per. | Total Revenue | Revenue Recognized (Current) |
|---|---|---|---|---|---|
| | | | | | |

| | Revenue Recognized (Current | Costs Incurred (Current) | Gross Profit Recognized (Current) |
|---|---|---|---|
| | | | |

#6 (a)

| | Cash Collected | Gross Profit Percentage | Gross Profit Recognized |
|---|---|---|---|
| | | | |

(b)

1.

2.

3.

Name

Section

Date



3. (Continued)

4.

5.

Name

Section

Date

**Problem 12-2A**

**Jose, Inc.**

1.

2.

3.

4.

5.

| Name | Problem 12-3A |
|---|---|
| Section | |
| Date | Rasheed Construction Company |

| Year | Current Period Costs | ÷ | Total Estimated Cost | = | Percent Complete | × | Total Revenue | = | Revenue Recognized (Current) |
|---|---|---|---|---|---|---|---|---|---|
| | | | | | | | | | |
| 1998 | | | | | | | | | |
| | | | | | | | | | |
| | | | | | | | | | |
| 1999 | | | | | | | | | |
| | | | | | | | | | |
| | | | | | | | | | |
| 2000 | | | | | | | | | |
| | | | | | | | | | |
| | | | | | | | | | |
| 2001 | | | | | | | | | |
| | | | | | | | | | |
| | | | | | | | | | |
| Totals | | | | | | | | | |
| | | | | | | | | | |

| Year | Revenue Recognized (Current) | − | Cost Incurred (Current) | = | Gross Profit Recognized (Current) |
|---|---|---|---|---|---|
| | | | | | |
| 1998 | | | | | |
| | | | | | |
| 1999 | | | | | |
| | | | | | |
| 2000 | | | | | |
| | | | | | |
| 2001 | | | | | |
| | | | | | |
| | | | | | |
| Totals | | | | | |
| | | | | | |

Name

Section

Date



| Year | Cash Collected | × | Gross Profit Percentage | = | Gross Profit Recognized |
|---|---|---|---|---|---|
| (a) | | | | | |
| 1998 | | | | | |
| | | | | | |
| 1999 | | | | | |
| | | | | | |
| 2000 | | | | | |
| | | | | | |
| | | | | | |
| Totals | | | | | |
| | | | | | |
| | | | | | |
| | | | | | |
| | | | | | |
| | | | | | |
| | | | | | |
| (b) | | | | | |
| 1998 | | | | | |
| | | | | | |
| 1999 | | | | | |
| | | | | | |
| 2000 | | | | | |
| | | | | | |
| | | | | | |
| Totals | | | | | |
| | | | | | |

Name

Section

Date

**Problem 12-5A**

1.

2.

3.

4.

5.

6.

7.

8.

Name

Section

Date

**Problem 12-1**

**Arruza Printers**

1.

2.

3.

3. (Continued)

4.

5.

6.

Name
Section
Date

**Problem 12-2B**

**Quester, Inc.**

1.

2.

3.

4.

5.

Name

Section

Date

**Problem 12-3B**

**Estafan Construction Company**

| Year | Current Period Costs ÷ | Total Estimated Cost = | Percent Complete × | Total Revenue = | Revenue Recognized (Current) |
|---|---|---|---|---|---|
| | | | | | |
| 1995 | | | | | |
| | | | | | |
| | | | | | |
| 1996 | | | | | |
| | | | | | |
| | | | | | |
| 1997 | | | | | |
| | | | | | |
| | | | | | |
| 1998 | | | | | |
| | | | | | |
| | | | | | |
| Totals | | | | | |
| | | | | | |

| Year | Revenue Recognized (Current) − | Cost Incurred (Current) = | Gross Profit Recognized (Current) |
|---|---|---|---|
| | | | |
| 1998 | | | |
| | | | |
| 1999 | | | |
| | | | |
| 2000 | | | |
| | | | |
| 2001 | | | |
| | | | |
| | | | |
| Totals | | | |
| | | | |

Name

Section

Date

**Problem 12-4B**

**Donovan, Inc.**

| Year | Cash Collected | × | Gross Profit Percentage | = | Gross Profit Recognized |
|---|---|---|---|---|---|
| (a) | | | | | |
| 1998 | | | | | |
| | | | | | |
| 1999 | | | | | |
| | | | | | |
| 2000 | | | | | |
| | | | | | |
| | | | | | |
| Totals | | | | | |
| | | | | | |
| | | | | | |
| | | | | | |
| | | | | | |
| | | | | | |
| | | | | | |
| (b) | | | | | |
| 1998 | | | | | |
| | | | | | |
| 1999 | | | | | |
| | | | | | |
| 2000 | | | | | |
| | | | | | |
| | | | | | |
| Totals | | | | | |
| | | | | | |

Name

Section

Date

**Problem 12-5B**

1.

2.

3.

4.

5.

6.

7.

8.

9.

(a)

(b)

(c)

(d)

Name

Section

Date

Wade Greaton

(e)

(f)

(g)

Name

Section

Date



(a)

1.

2.

3.

Name

Section

Date



**Margo Industries**

(b)

Talley Construction Division

Shumway Securities Division

**REAL-WORLD FOCUS** Newcor, Inc.

**ETHICS CASE** Mintur Corporation

Name

Section

Date

Name

Section

Date

ame

ection

ate

**Exercises 13-1, 13-3, and 13-4**

#1

#3

LED ZEPPELIN CO.
Partners' Capital Statement
For the Year Ended December 31, 1999

LED ZEPPELIN CO.
Balance Sheet (Partial)
December 31, 1999

Owners' Equity

#4

Name Exercise 13-

Section

Date Manilow and How Partnershi

(a) DIVISION OF NET INCOME

| | B. Manilow | W. How | Total |
|---|---|---|---|
| (1) Net income is $55,000: | | | |
| (2) Net income is $30,000: | | | |

(b)

| | | | | |
|---|---|---|---|---|
| (1) Net income is $55,000: | | | | |
| (2) Net income is $30,000: | | | | |

Name

Section

Date



#5

#6

Name

Section

Date

**Exercise 13-**

**Nagel, White, and Rundgren Partnershi**

1.

2.

Section

Date



THE PIPS COMPANY
Schedule of Cash Payments

| | Item | Cash | Non cash Assets | Liabilities | Gladys Capital | Knight Capital | |
|---|---|---|---|---|---|---|---|
| 1 | | | | | | | 1 |
| 2 | | | | | | | 2 |
| 3 | | | | | | | 3 |
| 4 | | | | | | | 4 |
| 5 | | | | | | | 5 |
| 6 | | | | | | | 6 |
| 7 | | | | | | | 7 |
| 8 | | | | | | | 8 |
| 9 | | | | | | | 9 |
| 10 | | | | | | | 10 |
| 11 | | | | | | | 11 |
| 12 | | | | | | | 12 |
| 13 | | | | | | | 13 |
| 14 | | | | | | | 14 |
| 15 | | | | | | | 15 |
| 16 | | | | | | | 16 |
| 17 | | | | | | | 17 |
| 18 | | | | | | | 18 |
| 19 | | | | | | | 19 |
| 20 | | | | | | | 20 |

Name

Section

Date



#9

#10

 

Name **Problem 13-1A**

Section

Date **Roberta Flack Company**

General Journal

| Date | Account Titles and Explanation | Ref. | Debit | Credit |
|---|---|---|---|---|
| (a) | | | | |
| (b) | | | | |

(c)

ROBERTA FLACK COMPANY
Balance Sheet
January 1, 1999

Assets

Liabilities and Owners' Equity

Name ______ **Problem 13-2A**

Section ______

Date ______ **LMC Company**

(a)

1.

2.

3.

(b)

LMC COMPANY
Division of Net Income

| | | Lois Lang | Mary Mio | Kim Casey | Total |
|---|---|---|---|---|---|
| 1 | | | | | |
| 2 | | | | | |
| 3 | | | | | |
| 4 | | | | | |
| 5 | | | | | |
| 6 | | | | | |
| 7 | | | | | |
| 8 | | | | | |
| 9 | | | | | |
| 10 | | | | | |
| 11 | | | | | |
| 12 | | | | | |
| 13 | | | | | |
| 14 | | | | | |
| 15 | | | | | |
| 16 | | | | | |
| 17 | | | | | |
| 18 | | | | | |
| 19 | | | | | |
| 20 | | | | | |

(c)

LMC COMPANY
Partners' Capital Statement
For the Year Ended December 31, 1999

| | | Lois Lang | Mary Mio | Kim Casey | Total |
|---|---|---|---|---|---|
| 1 | | | | | |
| 2 | | | | | |
| 3 | | | | | |
| 4 | | | | | |
| 5 | | | | | |
| 6 | | | | | |
| 7 | | | | | |
| 8 | | | | | |
| 9 | | | | | |
| 10 | | | | | |

Name

Section

Date

**Problem 13-3A**

**ELMO Company**

(a)

1.

2.

3.

(a) (Continued) and (b)

4.

(b)

Name

Section

Date

**Problem 13-4A**

**ART Company**

(a) 1.

2.

3.

4.

(b)

Name

Section

Date

**Problem 13-5A**

**Inland Lakes Company**

(a)

INLAND LAKES COMPANY
Schedule of Cash Payments

| | Item | Cash | Noncash Assets | Liabilities | T. E. Huron, Capital | P. A. Erie, Capital | C. R. Lake, Capital | |
|---|---|---|---|---|---|---|---|---|
| 1 | Balances before liquidation | 24000 | | | 24000 | 12800 | 3200 | 1 |
| 2 | | | | | | | | 2 |
| 3 | | | | | | | | 3 |
| 4 | | | | | | | | 4 |
| 5 | | | | | | | | 5 |
| 6 | | | | | | | | 6 |
| 7 | | | | | | | | 7 |
| 8 | | | | | | | | 8 |
| 9 | | | | | | | | 9 |
| 10 | | | | | | | | 10 |
| 11 | | | | | | | | 11 |
| 12 | | | | | | | | 12 |
| 13 | | | | | | | | 13 |
| 14 | | | | | | | | 14 |
| 15 | | | | | | | | 15 |

(c)

| Cash | |
|---|---|
| 4/30 Bal. 24,000 | |

| T. E. Huron, Capital | |
|---|---|
| | 4/30 Bal. 24,000 |

| P. A. Erie, Capital | |
|---|---|
| | 4/30 Bal. 12,800 |

| C. R. Lake, Capital | |
|---|---|
| | 4/30 Bal. 3,200 |

ame Problem 13-5A Concluded

ection

ate Inland Lakes Company

(b) General Journal

| Date | Account Titles and Explanation | Ref. | Debit | Credit |
|---|---|---|---|---|

Name **Problem 13-1**

Section

Date **Elvis Costello Compar**

General Journal

| | Date | Account Titles and Explanation | Ref. | Debit | Credit |
|---|---|---|---|---|---|
| 1 | (a) | | | | |
| 2 | | | | | |
| 3 | | | | | |
| 4 | | | | | |
| 5 | | | | | |
| 6 | | | | | |
| 7 | | | | | |
| 8 | | | | | |
| 9 | | | | | |
| 10 | | | | | |
| 11 | | | | | |
| 12 | | | | | |
| 13 | | | | | |
| 14 | | | | | |
| 15 | | | | | |
| 16 | | | | | |
| 17 | | | | | |
| 18 | | | | | |
| 19 | | | | | |
| 20 | | | | | |
| 21 | | | | | |
| 22 | | | | | |
| 23 | | | | | |
| 24 | | | | | |
| 25 | | | | | |
| 26 | (b) | | | | |
| 27 | | | | | |
| 28 | | | | | |
| 29 | | | | | |
| 30 | | | | | |
| 31 | | | | | |
| 32 | | | | | |
| 33 | | | | | |
| 34 | | | | | |
| 35 | | | | | |
| 36 | | | | | |
| 37 | | | | | |
| 38 | | | | | |
| 39 | | | | | |
| 40 | | | | | |

 

(c)

ELVIS COSTELLO COMPANY
Balance Sheet
January 1, 1999

| | |
|---|---|
| Assets | |
| | |
| | |
| | |
| | |
| | |
| | |
| | |
| | |
| | |
| | |
| | |
| | |
| | |
| | |
| Liabilities and Owners' Equity | |
| | |
| | |
| | |
| | |
| | |
| | |
| | |
| | |
| | |
| | |
| | |
| | |
| | |
| | |

 

Name

Section

Date

**Problem 13-2**

**HRZ Compan**

(a)

1.

2.

3.

(b)

HRZ COMPANY
Division of Net Income

| | Sue Hidalgo | Tracey Rugen | Eileen Zak | Total |
|---|---|---|---|---|
| | | | | |
| | | | | |
| | | | | |
| | | | | |
| | | | | |
| | | | | |
| | | | | |
| | | | | |
| | | | | |
| | | | | |
| | | | | |
| | | | | |
| | | | | |
| | | | | |
| | | | | |
| | | | | |
| | | | | |
| | | | | |
| | | | | |
| | | | | |

(c)

HRZ COMPANY
Partners' Capital Statement
For the Year Ended December 31, 1999

| | Sue Hidalgo | Tracey Rugen | Eileen Zak | Total |
|---|---|---|---|---|
| | | | | |
| | | | | |
| | | | | |
| | | | | |
| | | | | |
| | | | | |
| | | | | |
| | | | | |
| | | | | |
| | | | | |

Name

Section

Date

**Problem 13-3B**

**NSWO Company**

(a)

1.

2.

3.

Name

Section

Date



**NSWO Company**

(a) (Continued) and (b)

4.

(b)

Name

Section

Date

**Problem 13-4B**

**BAG Company**

(a) 1.

2.

3.

4.

(b)

Name **Problem 13-5B**

Section

Date **JRS Company**

(a)

Name

Section

Date



(b)

| Cash | |
|---|---|
| Bal. 27,500 | |

| M. Jagger, Capital | |
|---|---|
| | Bal. 35,000 |

| K. Richards, Capital | |
|---|---|
| | Bal. 20,000 |

| R. Simka, Capital | |
|---|---|
| | Bal. 1,200 |

(c)

| | | | | |
|---|---|---|---|---|
| 1 | | | | 1 |
| 2 | | | | 2 |
| 3 | | | | 3 |
| 4 | | | | 4 |
| 5 | | | | 5 |
| 6 | | | | 6 |
| 7 | | | | 7 |
| 8 | | | | 8 |
| 9 | | | | 9 |
| 10 | | | | 10 |
| 11 | | | | 11 |
| 12 | | | | 12 |
| 13 | | | | 13 |
| 14 | | | | 14 |
| 15 | | | | 15 |
| 16 | | | | 16 |
| 17 | | | | 17 |
| 18 | | | | 18 |
| 19 | | | | 19 |
| 20 | | | | 20 |

Name

Section

Date

**Chapter 12 Group Decision Case**

**Homar Izod Partnership**

(a)

(b)

(c)

(d)

(e)

Name

Section

Date



**REAL-WORLD FOCUS** Texas Meridian Resources

(a)

(b)

(c)

Name

Section

Date

**ETHICS CASE** Susan and Karen Partnership

(a)

(b)

(c)

Name 

Section

Date

Name **Exercise D-1**

Section

Date **Cecilie Company**

(a)

CECILIE COMPANY

Income Statement (Partial)

For the Year Ended October 31, 1999

(b) General Journal

| Date | Account Titles and Explanations | Debit | Credit |
|---|---|---|---|
| | Closing Entries | | |

Name

Section

Date

**Exercises D-2**

**L. Pele Company**

General Journal

| Date | Account Titles and Explanation | Debit | Credit |
|---|---|---|---|
| (a) | | | |
| (b) | Closing Entries | | |

Name

Section

Date

**Exercise D-**

**G. Garbo Company**

(a) Cost of goods sold

(b) Closing Entries

(c)

MERCHANDISE INVENTORY

Name — Exercise D-4

Section

Date — **B. Milia Company**

B. MILIA COMPANY
Work Sheet (Partial)
For the Period Ended May 31, 1999

(a)

| | Account Titles | Adjusted Trial Balance Dr. | Adjusted Trial Balance Cr. | Income Statement Dr. | Income Statement Cr. | Balance Sheet Dr. | Balance Sheet Cr. | |
|---|---|---|---|---|---|---|---|---|
| 1 | | | | | | | | 1 |
| 2 | Cash | 9000 | | | | | | 2 |
| 3 | Merchandise Inventory | 80000 | | | | | | 3 |
| 4 | Purchases | 240000 | | | | | | 4 |
| 5 | Purchase Returns and Allowances | | 30000 | | | | | 5 |
| 6 | Sales | | 450000 | | | | | 6 |
| 7 | Sales Returns and Allowances | 10000 | | | | | | 7 |
| 8 | Sales Discounts | 5000 | | | | | | 8 |
| 9 | Rent Expense | 42000 | | | | | | 9 |
| 10 | | | | | | | | 10 |
| 11 | | | | | | | | 11 |
| 12 | | | | | | | | 12 |
| 13 | | | | | | | | 13 |
| 14 | | | | | | | | 14 |
| 15 | | | | | | | | 15 |

(b)

| | | |
|---|---|---|
| 1 | | 1 |
| 2 | | 2 |
| 3 | | 3 |

Additional working papers for this problem are at the back of this book.

(b)

MESA WHOLESALE COMPANY
Income Statement
For the Year Ended December 31, 1999

Name

Section

Date

**Problem D-1 Continued**

**Mesa Wholesale Company**

(b) (Continued)

MESA WHOLESALE COMPANY

Owner's Equity Statement

For the Year Ended December 31, 1999

MESA WHOLESALE COMPANY

Balance Sheet

December 31, 1999

Assets

Liabilities and Owner's Equity

Name

Section

Date

**Problem D-1 Continued**

**Mesa Wholesale Company**

(c) and (d) General Journal

| Date | Account Titles and Explanation | Debit | Credit |
|---|---|---|---|
| (c) | Adjusting Entries | | |
| (d) | Closing Entries | | |

Name

Section

Date

**Problem D-1 Concluded**

**Mesa Wholesale Company**

(d) (Continued)

General Journal

| | Date | Account Titles and Explanation | Debit | Credit | |
|---|---|---|---|---|---|
| 1 | | | | | 1 |
| 2 | | | | | 2 |
| 3 | | | | | 3 |
| 4 | | | | | 4 |
| 5 | | | | | 5 |
| 6 | | | | | 6 |
| 7 | | | | | 7 |
| 8 | | | | | 8 |
| 9 | | | | | 9 |
| 10 | | | | | 10 |
| 11 | | | | | 11 |
| 12 | | | | | 12 |
| 13 | | | | | 13 |
| 14 | | | | | 14 |
| 15 | | | | | 15 |

(e)

MESA WHOLESALE COMPANY
Post-Closing Trial Balance
December 31, 1999

| | | Debit | Credit | |
|---|---|---|---|---|
| 1 | | | | 1 |
| 2 | | | | 2 |
| 3 | | | | 3 |
| 4 | | | | 4 |
| 5 | | | | 5 |
| 6 | | | | 6 |
| 7 | | | | 7 |
| 8 | | | | 8 |
| 9 | | | | 9 |
| 10 | | | | 10 |
| 11 | | | | 11 |
| 12 | | | | 12 |
| 13 | | | | 13 |
| 14 | | | | 14 |
| 15 | | | | 15 |
| 16 | | | | 16 |
| 17 | | | | 17 |
| 18 | | | | 18 |

Name

Section

Date

**Problem D-2 Continued**

**Ivanna Fashion Center**

Additional working papers for this problem are at the back of this book.

(b)

IVANNA FASHION CENTER

Income Statement

For the Year Ended November 30, 1999

(b) (Continued)

IVANNA FASHION CENTER
Owner's Equity Statement
For the Year Ended December 31, 1999

IVANNA FASHION CENTER
Balance Sheet
December 31, 1999

Assets

Liabilities and Owner's Equity

Name

Section

Date

**Problem D-2 Continue**

**Ivanna Fashion Cent**

General Journal

| Date | Account Titles and Explanation | Debit | Credit |
|---|---|---|---|
| (c) | Adjusting Entries | | |
| (d) | Closing Entries | | |

(d) (Continued)

General Journal

| Date | Account Titles and Explanation | Debit | Credit |
|---|---|---|---|

(e)

IVANNA FASHION CENTER
Post-Closing Trial Balance
November 30, 1999

| | Debit | Credit |
|---|---|---|

Name

Section

Date

**Problem D-3 Continued**

**World Enterprises**

Additional working papers for this problem are at the back of this book.

(b) and (c) General Journal

| Date | Account Titles and Explanation | Debit | Credit |
|---|---|---|---|
| (b) | Adjusting Entries | | |
| (c) | Closing Entries | | |

Name

Section

Date

**Problem D-3 Concluded**

**World Enterprises**

(d)

MERCHANDISE INVENTORY

INCOME SUMMARY